PEOPLE-CENTRIC MANAGEMENT

HOW MANAGERS USE FOUR LEVERS TO BRING OUT THE GREATNESS OF OTHERS

LUKAS MICHEL

ADVANCE PRAISE

"In this important and highly readable book, Lukas Michel once again draws on his extensive consulting experience and his deep knowledge of key academic theories and figures. He connects the dots in a way that gives business agility even more meaning. The result is another strong confirmation that the future of management must be and will be people-centric."

Bjarte Bogsnes
Chairman, Beyond Budgeting Roundtable, London

"In *People-Centric Management*, Lukas Michel describes a style of management that responds to the complexities of our time with flexibility and humanity. He diagnoses the challenges of modern businesses succinctly, noting the increase of volatility, uncertainty, complexity and ambiguity (VUCA) as a hallmark of our time. He reminds us how current business practice relies on a kind of stability that no longer exists, and he contrasts agile practices with traditional ones simply and clearly. Agile managers, in his view, help others to know with clarity, to move in one direction, to mobilize energy, and to maintain focus. In each of these areas, he identifies the key tensions that managers face and outlines an operating system, a set of considerations, that managers can use to address the tensions. Throughout, he demonstrates his deep expertise of how people in organizations understand and act in their environment. Michel is gentle but clear in his criticism of traditional practice: change is not optional, it is essential. In *People-Centric Management* managers will find clear guidance to their pressing business problems: become agile to remain humane."

Dr Fritz Gugelmann
Director, Business Development,
Duke Corporate Education Durham, Durham NC

"Lukas Michel's new book recognizes that most management thinking is 'utopian, untested and has limited theoretical underpinning, and is of little use to practitioners.' He redresses the balance with a careful, tested, system of thinking about your business that should bring results. He does not tell you what to do. There are plenty of books on what to do, most of which are padded with examples, none of which, however inspiring, bear any direct relation to the reader's circumstances. He tells you how to do it. It will make you work, not just read. That work will be helpful to your understanding of how your organization functions, where it can improve and how to get there."

Nick Hixson
CEO, Hixsons Limited, Bournemouth

Published by
LID Publishing Limited
The Record Hall, Studio 304,
16-16a Baldwins Gardens,
London EC1N 7RJ, UK

info@lidpublishing.com
www.lidpublishing.com

A member of:

BPR ⊛
businesspublishersroundtable.com

Printed in the United States

ISBN: 978-1-912555-99-4
ISBN: 978-1-911671-17-6 (ebook)

Cover and page design: Caroline Li

PEOPLE-CENTRIC MANAGEMENT

HOW MANAGERS USE FOUR LEVERS TO BRING OUT THE GREATNESS OF OTHERS

LUKAS MICHEL

MADRID | MEXICO CITY | LONDON
NEW YORK | BUENOS AIRES
BOGOTA | SHANGHAI | NEW DELHI

CONTENTS

To my wife Charleen and her support.

ACKNOWLEDGMENTS

People-Centric Management is the result of 20 years of work with clients around the globe, the rich exchange with members of the AGILITYINSIGHTS network and my annual visits every fall to the Global Drucker Forum in Vienna.

My thanks to our clients for their ongoing support. They've lived through prototypes of our diagnostics and models, and have helped us develop our mentoring tools to where they are today.

The members of our mentoring network have been part of the development of this book. Special thanks to Raymond Hofmann, Günther Kopperger, Michael Eckert, Mariola Czechowska-Frączak and Chander Nagpal for their considerable feedback. The research team, with Prof Dr Herb Nold and Prof Dr Johanna Anzengruber, has extensively published on the models and diagnostics. Without their work, this book would not have the solid ground and backing in research it now has.

My special thanks go to Johanna. She has offered her wise insights from the younger generation of leaders and her kind nudges on the levers we jointly developed. It's fair to say that she has made me switch to people-centric.

My thanks also go to all associates from the Peter Drucker Forum, including management researchers, businesspeople and consulting colleagues who have challenged my thinking by offering their ideas and concerns. In particular, my thanks go to Dr Richard Straub, who has been a kind supporter for the last ten years.

My final thanks are for my wife, Charleen. She has supported my work for years, and helpfully relaxed some of my daily household duties.

Lukas Michel
St Moritz, January 2020

FOREWORD

We all love stories, and this is the perfect book to help you generate your transition story.

It is also an invitation to reflect on your own practices, as well as the practices of others in leading organizations. This book aims to guide those readers who are open to experiencing Lukas Michel's world of thoughts and ideas.

He gently brings leadership, management and managerial psychology perspectives together by introducing a variety of known and lesser-known leadership instruments and mindsets. He also provides a summary of all his previously published work. This new book is especially designed as a set of practice guidelines, to help you find your own individual path to what he calls 'People-Centric Management.'

For almost ten years now, we have both been on a mission to spread the enabling and self-organized paradigm among public and private organizations, academia and university students, helping individuals, teams and firms on their journey towards it. Over the years, we have come to an understanding: There is much to do!

For instance, it was only recently that a high-ranking government official proudly told me that she had punished a subordinate (also a high-ranking government official) because he was – in her mind – spending too much time teaching lower-ranked staff. Clearly, such behaviours put a heavy burden on people who have already incorporated the enabling mode as their way of living and leading, while the establishment continues to proudly fight for the survival of command and control.

In a recent study among traditional companies, we found that this state of mind unfortunately exists on a large scale. In a nutshell, it revealed that leaders showing higher enabling capabilities than their peers are often undervalued and underrated by their bosses.

These are just two examples of a long list of similar instances that happen around the globe every day. This makes it necessary to mobilize as much energy as possible to shift the mindset towards the dual mode and create a whole generation of natural-born enablers.

This book offers a great opportunity to learn how to make such a shift.

I would recommend flipping to the end of the book and doing your diagnostics before you actually start reading. Your diagnostics will provide you with greater awareness, focus and clarity, as well as more opportunities for future self-enabled actions!

Prof Dr Johanna Anzengruber
Vienna, January 2020

PREFACE

In this book, I argue that People-Centric Management is essential to succeed in the new dynamic business context. It proposes four people-centric levers that unlock the full potential of people to operate in a mode that balances efficiency with innovation.

Why are people the centre of attention in this book? To release their talent and succeed in a dynamic context, people need a work environment that differs from traditional organizations. They need one with managers who share a mindset, skill set and toolset designed for people. It caters to the individual, and its design has the potential to scale.

Why another book? One could argue the following: (1) There's plenty of research featured in professional publications on the new context, with recipes for better management. (2) Digital, agile, new work, reinventing, transformation, and many more attributes are trendy. They figure prominently in social media. There is an abundance of advice, conferences and workouts – some call it 'work out loud' – available. And, there is more to come. (3) Thousands of books are published annually on leadership attributes, agility and people, but few on management, the essential social practice that makes organizations function. (4) Few publications combine people-centric and agile. This combination needs to be made explicit, and it's different from 'managing people,' which requires a different mindset and capabilities. While this is a management book, it focuses on what all executives need to put in place as their art, science and craft to bring out the best in people and make others successful.

The idea for *People-Centric Management* has its roots in the academic Sumantra Ghoshal's seminal article, 'Bad Management Theories Are Destroying Good Management Practice.' "Our theories and ideas have done much to strengthen the management practices that we are all now so loudly condemning," he wrote in 2005.

He refers to ideas espoused by business schools 30 years ago, such as agency theory, transaction costs and competitive strategy, and calls them 'negative theories.' Their underlying assumptions are that people need motivation to do things; control and tight monitoring is required; and businesses must be competitive in nature to survive. Negative problems then focus on how organizations need to be managed to prevent 'bad' people from doing harm to others. He says these ideas have dominated much of past management research and practice.

We've reached a critical tipping point for management, and it needs to change. The dynamic contexts in which most businesses operate demand innovation more than efficiency, the latter of which looks for better, dynamic ways of managing and organizing. In modern ecosystems, cooperation beats competition. Savvy businesses are built on the assumption that self-responsible people, self-organization and collaboration are the means to deliver customer value. It's a whole new world for most managers, and research is picking up on early examples of the new practices.

My hope is that *People-Centric Management* will help you make the transition from the traditional paradigm to better ways of doing things. The challenge for most leaders is to balance the tensions between the changing business context, prevailing traditional management approaches and the needs of people to apply their potential.

In that sense, the concept of People-Centric Management offers a choice, with levers, management modes and operating systems that help you find your own approach to managing your business. This applies to large corporations, small to medium-sized enterprises (SMEs), start-ups or non-profit organizations, in all sectors.

Many management theories have passed their time. They were developed for a stable economy but remain sticky. Efficiency, the hallmark of traditional management, still dominates for one reason: it is easy to measure and to apply, despite the fact that it ignores social cost in favour of economic benefits. There is no doubt that efficiency is a necessary feature in every business. But, there are other features that become equally, if not more, important.

New theories are under construction, and businesses are experimenting with new ways of operating. I will summarize the new theories and features with the 'agile' label, and will use 'traditional' to describe what most of us know from our own experience of working in bureaucratic organizations. To refine the analysis of agile, I will add 'people-centric' and 'dynamic' qualities. People-centric describes the managerial principles of how we lead people in the knowledge era. Dynamic adds the features of how we design the managerial operating system for a dynamic business environment.

For purposes of *People-Centric Management*, I define agile as a broad, dynamic capability and philosophy that helps organizations compete in a dynamic business environment, and helps people to apply their full talent in serving customers. Agile comes with its own managerial style, organizational features, and operating toolbox.

As a managerial and institutional capability, agile spans the entire organization. With the four people-centric levers, and if done correctly, agile turns into an individual capability, and a scalable one, for each person and for the organization as a whole. With agile fully scaled up, it is then every manager's task to establish a work environment that meets the needs of people, the context of their organization, and the specific challenges and business opportunities of the job to be done.

No one model fits all. As such, agile has a design for people. Once designed, managers and employees need the rights and skills to effectively apply people-centric principles in practice. In combination, agile, people-centric and dynamic capabilities are prerequisites for individual and institutional peak performance. They are the features that help business turn opportunity into value.

I share your frustrations. With few exceptions, popular management literature is utopian, untested, has a limited theoretical underpinning, and much of it is of little use for practitioners. Self-appointed utopians, exorcists, and messiahs abound, offering the next new trend that waits just around the corner.

It's hard to deal with contradictory concepts and to separate the noise from what works in practice. Simple recipes, best practices, tips and easy solutions don't work. Adding new attributes to leadership – and guiding executives with 'new,' 'reinventing' and 'disruptive' management and organizational theories – is of little help. 'Copy & paste' means averaging in on others. The result is mediocrity. Simply adding 'digital' to everything is not helpful either.

People-Centric Management is grounded in solid management research and 20 years of application in professional settings. It offers a learning journey based on executive experience. The quality of learning depends on your ability to focus your attention, and success comes from applying your own experience through doing rather than talking. Wise management advice is rare and limited to a handful of management authors. By engaging in the annual Global Drucker Forum in Vienna over the past years, I've been able to gain insider access to many globally renowned management experts. Every personal encounter was a memorable experience, and much of this has found its way into this book.

I also understand why it's hard to leave traditional approaches. Few leaders are willing to abandon their comfort zone for the chaos of uncharted territory. It's a risk. And the Dunning-Kruger effect (Dunning, 2011) points to many leaders overestimating their own capabilities, and those of their organization, in making the shift. As a leader, self-confidence is essential; it is part of any leader's DNA. But overconfidence and risk-aversity are like boomerangs. Demotivation and the feeling that change is impossible spread like a virus in teams. That leader gets very lonely, giving rise to the conviction that it's the leader who has to do all the work. And so, there we are, stuck in a vicious circle.

Conversely, People-Centric Management promotes a team approach. You start with a diagnostic process, and then have the team design and share the development work. It is the means to counteract overestimation and risk-bias effects.

The shift from traditional to people-centric changes the paradigm of how we organize, manage and lead. Agile and dynamic are complimentary and context-specific capabilities. They come with different assumptions about people that have an impact on the role of management. The shift calls for scaling these capabilities throughout an entire organization. Scaling agile, people-centric and dynamic capabilities is a deep transformation. With clarity on the design, these capabilities need practice. Experience expedites the learning. Therefore, the shift is a transformation that changes traditional management paradigms. It is not another quick-fix project.

Managers are used to discussing marketing, sales and manufacturing. These are conversations on hard topics. On the other hand, conversations about people-centric, agile and management are soft and fuzzy. A framework is needed to initiate soft conversation, such that all parties feel safe. This book offers that kind of a framing, with a valid model that offers options, diagnostics for discovery and guidance on the shift, along with proven steps to take.

We have crossed the Rubicon. Most organizations recognize the need for new ways of managing. However, many struggle with translating a 20-year old software development concept into a broader management and organization practice. In our 2018 global study on agile management, which included 250 organizations of every size and type, we learned that 80% of executive teams agreed that agile capabilities matter. Yet, only 20% of the same executives claimed that they were actively introducing agile. The difference in agile capabilities between bottom-tier and top-tier organizations, as measured on our Agile Maturity scale, is nearly 50%. Many other independent studies reveal a similar state of agile.

There is much to do. Action needs to follow talk. It's time for strategic agile, with a design for people and a scale beyond its original scope in IT. That's what People-Centric Management helps you achieve.

In this book, we illustrate how leaders can raise awareness (decode and understand agile), grow insights (make choices about a people-centric design) and facilitate learning (develop these capabilities at scale). We show how they can then apply (lead the people-centric way) people-centric practices that enable people to find purpose, build relationships and intensively collaborate for greatness in a dynamic context.

The notion of People-Centric Management has grown out of our practice with clients, my experiences with my previous books and the research that guided the development of this book. Many clients have experienced how to make people-centric work through agile capabilities. *The Performance Triangle* articulated the agile model in response to a dynamic environment, with the elements that make up an agile organization. *Management Design* offered the methodology and process for developing agile capabilities. *Agile by Choice* provided nudges to guide agile development. Our continued research on agile, people-centric and dynamic capabilities[1] convinced me that it was now time to write about People-Centric Management. My friends know that the last thing I would ever write about is leadership. And so, here we are: it's about management. It is a book on the necessary design requirements for people-centric, with a guide on how to get there. Most would call it leadership stuff. For me, it's another contribution to better management seen as an art, a science and a practice, as the work of management theorists Peter Drucker and Henry Mintzberg keeps reminding us.

In that sense, this is a practical guide for leaders (those who have the freedom and choice to decide and act for themselves) to make the shift to people-centric. I never said that this is easy. It's conceptual in nature. And, it's up to the reader to apply the principles to the specifics of his or her situation. All I ask is that you do it right from the beginning: raise awareness, act on the insights and accelerate the learning.

People-Centric Management is about decoding, designing and developing capabilities at scale. It's about asking how you, as a leader, can ensure that people throughout the organization: unlock their full talent; capture the benefits of the new context (digital, fast, agile, resilient); and become effective in dealing with an adverse business context (complex, uncertain, ambiguous, and volatile). At the same time, it's about exploring how you develop management and organization with a culture, leadership and systems that create a work environment conducive to people succeeding.

People-centric comes with four questions to guide you on your way to capture and exploit business opportunities:

1. **What is my purpose?** Individual people-centric relies on a shared understanding of context and purpose for people to identify valuable business opportunities.
2. **Who and what can I rely on?** People-centric on a shared intent with a broad set of ambitions for people to select valuable business opportunities.
3. **What support do I get and offer?** People-centric at scale relies on a shared agenda with the energy and resources needed for people to turn valuable business opportunities into value for customers.
4. **How do I stay on track?** Individual agility at scale also relies on shared beliefs and boundaries, which help people to not get distracted and stick with the chosen business opportunities, delivering long-term value for society.

Chapter 1 outlines the trends, opportunities and risks of the new, digital business context. We discuss the tensions between the challenges and capabilities needed to address the new context.

Chapter 2 offers four levers, with a choice of principles to reconcile the tensions. These choices are the keys to identifying the means and operating systems, with a design that fits the needs of people and the specific business context.

Chapters 3-6 introduce each of the four levers, with options on principles, means and systems relative to *what* managers can do to capture opportunities, despite the challenges of their context. As such, Chapter 3 identifies the principles of how people understand, as a means to address complexity. Chapter 4 describes alternative thinking on getting people to move in one direction. Chapter 5 introduces action, the ways to mobilize the energies to collaborate. Chapter 6 discusses two final principles that are needed to maintain focus in a volatile business context. The implications of these choices on the organization's operating system, leadership and culture are examined.

These capabilities do not work in isolation. Altering capabilities in one area impacts choices in another. And so, Chapter 7 offers a framework, with four managerial modes that align the levers and integrate them into powerful responses: four operating modes that fit the desired context.

In line with enabling mode, Chapter 8 offers the Performance Triangle model and the Leadership Scorecard, with 20 questions that can help leaders initiate the shift to people-centric.

Chapters 9-11 outline what it takes to develop people-centric. Chapter 9 offers four shifts that establish people-centric, and a dynamic toolbox to make it work. Chapter 10 frames the dual operating system, with people-centric at its core. Chapter 11 guides the transformation in three steps.

And finally, Chapter 12 provides some valuable ideas on how people-centric, agile and dynamic capabilities help managers achieve greatness through step-changes in a dynamic context.

By reading this book, you will learn how People-Centric Management and dynamic operating systems add to agile organization to emerge as the:

Principles that reconcile challenges, capabilities and opportunities

Elements of the agile Performance Triangle model

Means of work and prerequisite for customer focus

Levers and choice to bridge traditional and people-centric capabilities

Bridge between people, organization and context

Capacity to operate in hybrid contextual modes

Requirements for the design of the dynamic operating system

Features of the operating systems to combine scaling and individualizing

Insights you need to personally make the shift to people-centric

Guide for the transformation at scale

Qualities of management that help develop greatness in people

By the time you've finished reading this book, we are convinced that you will buy into the idea that People-Centric Management with agile and dynamic capabilities is the key to success in a dynamic environment. If you operate in a stable environment, then people-centric, agile and dynamic will separate you from the rest.

People-Centric Management follows Drucker's and Mintzberg's advice. My paramount motivation here is to support chiefs, executives, officers and leaders around the world in putting people back into management, a notion that's been lost over the past 50 years.

CHAPTER

THE NEW
BUSINESS
CONTEXT

PEOPLE-CENTRIC MANAGEMENT

Before digging into the *what* and the *how* of People-Centric Management, it is essential to understand *why* we need to care about agile – the capability that makes people-centric happen. It's because businesses today operate in a context that is fundamentally different from the past. Identifying valuable business opportunities and extracting value from them is more demanding than ever.

In this context, managers face challenges and opportunities that fundamentally alter the context in which they operate.[2] Competitive advantage has always been the ultimate goal of organizations. At their core is the need to perform and deliver value for their stakeholders. Transaction costs have been the drivers for competitive advantage, with the underlying assumption that business can control information in a stable environment. In such a context, traditional control-based management delivers the expected outcomes. However, unlike in previous centuries, information costs have decreased dramatically, enabling loosely-connected networks of professionals to remotely perform and create value.

Traditional organizations and management are barriers to achieving competitive advantage in a dynamic environment. Since many organizations today face higher 'volatility, uncertainty, complexity and ambiguity' (VUCA), an operating model is needed that can deliver the expected outcomes in a dynamic context. Traditional organizations were built for stability, efficiency and control. With the dynamic context, the focus has shifted to faster learning and innovation. No company can control all resources needed for innovation. Therefore, organizations increasingly need collaborative approaches, often with resources from outside the firm. As a consequence, organizations need to adapt their operations modes to the dynamics of the external environment.

We are at the inflection point where agile augments tradition. Two trends, digitalization and the reduction of information costs, fundamentally change the nature of work, how we organize and how we lead people.

Digitalization lowers information costs and enables new forms of interaction. Today, information is readily available, large amounts of data can be processed quickly, and communications technologies enable remote work. With readily available information, organizations can gain new insights, capture opportunities early and mitigate risks promptly. The dramatic reduction of information costs shifts work from being purely material and physical to something much more knowledge-oriented. Information search, knowledge creation and learning call for engaging the know-how and skills of remotely situated people who are driven by self-determination and self-organization.

Such decentralized, collaborative and self-organized management styles are in sharp contrast with traditional approaches dominated by managers. When work requires the knowledge of employees, teams and communities, People-Centric Management dominates. In such modern contexts, traditional formal control approaches lose their function. The ease of communications permits management styles rooted in free choice, sharing, transparency and the absence of rigid structures.

The new context (Figure 1) distinguishes between traditional and agile. In a traditional context, leaders focus on evaluating transaction outcomes and how well employees adhere to organizational rules and processes. Traditional bureaucratic control approaches emphasize the specification, monitoring and enforcement of rules and processes. Machines are good at efficiency and enable businesses to further exploit value.

Traditional		Agile
Stable Environment	Our context	Dynamic Environment
Operational Excellence	Our core process	Innovation
Exploitation	Our business model	Exploration
Traditional	← █ →	**Agile**
Control	How we lead	Enabling
Targets	How we engage people	Purpose
Transactions	What we value	Knowledge
Tangible	What we measure	Intangible
Education	How we learn	Experience

FIGURE 1: THE NEW CONTEXT

Agile capabilities in a fast moving, volatile and uncertain environment differ greatly from those in a stable context, where control dominates. When knowledge is important, a work environment that enables people to effectively apply their knowledge is fundamentally different from one where work is highly standardized, and managers can take control. Human beings are really good at most complex, collaborative and creative work. They are much better at this than machines. The VUCA part is hard for machines. This is the context where teams and organizations of human beings, working together towards a common goal, can create immense value.

The ability to create a work environment where people can contribute to breaking down bureaucracy and hierarchy, no matter who they are and what they do, allows for self-organization, enabling organizations to explore new value and grow.

Agile offers the capabilities needed to succeed in such a dynamic context. It's the prerequisite for People-Centric Management based on self-responsibility, self-organization and delegated decision-making through attention. In return, people-centric becomes the capacity that enables businesses to operate in more than one mode at a time.

The extent of external challenges and the distribution of knowledge are the two main triggers that raise the demand for agile capabilities with a people-centric approach.

THE DEGREE OF THE EXTERNAL CHALLENGES

In a stable environment, control dominates. Leaders refine their decision-making and planning as a stable platform from where they decide, act and control as the situation requires. With increasing complexity, ambiguity, uncertainty and volatility, agile approaches are necessary to quickly adapt to the new environment.

COMPLEXITY

Complexity increases with size. In established businesses, detailed home-grown processes and bureaucratic structures increase complexity. But as organizations grow and add complexity, the coordination of activities becomes increasingly important. Self-inflicted complexity is the result of *more of everything*, from the number of employees and operating locations to products on the shelf, segments served, functions performed and stakeholders with interests.

In a complex context, it is hard to understand – to hear weak signals, identify opportunities and be clear about what matters – and to find purpose. But when we lack clarity, we ask for additional detail and more precise processes. We introduce additional bureaucracy, applying rules and coordinating procedures that work well in simple contexts. Complexity cannot be compacted. It cannot be addressed through methodologies. Self-organization through teams beats bureaucracy in complex contexts.

AMBIGUITY

Ambiguity requires choice. Rules of the game change, markets evolve, certainties dissolve, industries merge and change, loyalty vanishes, taboos are broken and boundaries blur.

With increasing ambiguity, developing strategies and setting direction based on unpredictability and a variety of contextual settings requires information and knowledge. But when ambiguity creeps up, we set new rules and limit the degrees of freedom. We reinforce stability because we know how to deal with that. In ambiguous contexts, it is hard to decide – to select valuable opportunities and move in one direction. Relationships with those who know are needed. Ambiguity cannot be ruled, and in that context, delegation beats power. As such, seeing through ambiguity requires natural, team-based approaches as opposed to rational steps and simple models.

UNCERTAINTY

Uncertainty challenges strategy. Challenges to stability include shorter life cycles, less stable results, higher dependencies, more transparency and higher reputation risks, particularly those that appear suddenly.

In an uncertain context, it's hard to act and collaborate (i.e., turn opportunities into benefits). The risks of failure are high. But when uncertainty rises, we second-guess ourselves, mistrust people and limit delegation. We give orders and prevent the use of knowledge. In a stable, certain context, power and authority work well to get things done. Uncertainty cannot be controlled. But self-responsibility beats command and order. Digitalization helps to decentralize decision-making without losing control. As such, uncertainty demands trusted management and non-linear approaches.

VOLATILITY

Higher volatility is the norm in this day and age. Globalization, speed, real-time processes, faster decisions, synchronization and immediate responses are required.

In a highly dynamic context, flexibility is needed. Efficiency and scale require rigid routines for consistency and quality that work well in a stable context. But when control fails, we implement more of it. We double down with the tools and reinforce alignment. In a volatile environment, it's hard to maintain the focus on what truly matters, such as sticking with the opportunities. Narrow targets are always off. As such, attention beats detailed targets.

THE DISTRIBUTION OF KNOWLEDGE

Business is about exploiting valuable opportunities and turning them into client benefits. This requires information and knowledge: the second trigger.

When knowledge is concentrated, control, command and central decision-making dominate. The speed of decisions and the flexibility for action depends on the ability to search for information and the available knowledge.

When knowledge is widely distributed, managers engage people to collaborate and connect to build relationships, all with a deep sense of purpose. Complex structures are replaced by self-organized teams. They use inexpensive information and communications technologies in remote workplaces to detect opportunities early and act on weak market signals.

Four questions guide agile work:
- What is my purpose?
- Who and what can I rely on?
- What support do I get and offer?
- How do I stay on track?

Information and knowledge to identify, select, transform and exploit valuable opportunities that benefit stakeholders are the best means to address the challenges of a VUCA environment where knowledge is widely distributed. This is because:
- Clarity helps identify opportunities
- Direction helps with the selection of valuable opportunities
- Energy is needed to turn opportunities into value
- Focus is about sticking with the chosen opportunities

People who are successful at constantly searching for and uncovering new opportunities generally know with clarity, move in one direction, mobilize their energy and maintain their focus.

With the *knowledge worker* generation entering managerial jobs, the distinction between managers and employees increasingly vanishes. To quote Drucker, "With the knowledge age, employees become executives. They make decisions."[3] This is why, for purposes of this book, I often use 'people' to include leaders, managers, executives and employees.

THE MANAGERIAL OPERATING SYSTEM

In any organization, management operates on a system that enables people to get work done. Such a managerial operating system – with routines, rules, tools and a culture – facilitates interactions and creates a shared way of doing things. Think of the operating system in a computer: it makes the hardware work, to enable users to perform their tasks. In that sense, the managerial operating system does the same with organizations and people. It's the primary responsibility of managers to establish an operating system that suits the people, the purpose and the context of their business.

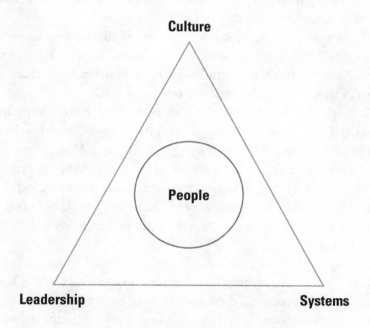

FIGURE 2: THE PERFORMANCE TRIANGLE

The Performance Triangle (Figure 2) represents the managerial operating system (with rules, routines and tools) to facilitate leadership and support people (with interaction skills). It also helps establish a shared culture (mindsets), be it for one's own firm, organization, unit or team, or as part of a farther-flung network, community, larger firm, organization, unit or team.

The triangle establishes performance through operations that facilitate learning as an opportunity, a capability and a state of readiness. The systems scientist Peter Senge (1990) put it as follows: "In a learning organization, leaders are designers, stewards, and teachers. They are responsible for building organizations where people continually expand their capabilities to understand complexity, clarify vision, and improve shared mental models – that is, they are responsible for learning."[4]

An organization's operating system needs to establish the opportunity to learn. It's the responsibility of the organization to offer the learning opportunity. The skill set is the prerequisite for the ability to learn. The role of leadership is to unlock the talent; the goal is to engage the capability to perform. It's a shared responsibility between the organization and the individual.

The mindset is a prerequisite for the ability to act. It enables learning and the application of skills. Culture creates the context for readiness. But it's every individual's responsibility to learn and engage, and to remain in a state of readiness.

Throughout history, operating systems have been increasingly challenged. Trust in systems is breaking down. And this is not unique to business – it's happening everywhere. More often than not, current discussions in politics and business challenge systems. We see political campaigns in modern democracies where candidates propose that public administration systems be torn down, claiming they aren't effective, are too expensive, have too many rules, limit freedom, etc.

Thousands of books are written every year that claim to add yet another attribute to leadership. They promise to provide 'the key to success,' 'the five recipes,' 'the ultimate goal,' etc. Leadership without systems does not work. Systems without leadership are meaningless. And systems without the right design by their managers don't effectively support leadership and people. Priest and management author Peter Scholtes (1998) put it this way: "Changing the system will change what people do. Changing what people do will not change the system ... Yet because we don't understand systems, we act as though human errors were the primary cause of our problems."[5]

Culture matters. Culture represents the set of formal and informal social norms in an organization. It is in the organization's interest to establish these norms in ways that enable people to cooperate in support of the overall performance goals. Culture provides what systems naturally cannot: the invisible, cooperative glue where performance targets, incentives, imperfect monitoring and sanctions are based on the negative assumptions of people; and a solution to the 'free-ride' problem. One should not be surprised that cultures quickly turn sour and become infected by viruses.

We often see new CEOs demanding radical culture change, in hope of better performance and service for clients. This means there's a need for a new and different system to scale and govern decision-making, actions and behaviours throughout an organization. A collaborative culture starts with positive assumptions about people, dynamic systems built in support of people and People-Centric Management.

Every organization needs its operating system to ensure effective business conduct. The general critique that questions the need of systems per se is inadequate and misses the point. If a car does not perform to expectation, nobody would challenge the essence of cars in general. We know from our research that most culture issues, faulty leadership or sub-par performance originates from an erroneous operating system. If something produces errors, it needs to be fixed or exchanged. The critique, properly addressed, may demand a reset, an update, a change or replacement of an organization's operating system.

Agile requires a different operating system. As we'll further explore in Chapter 10, both fixing and exchanging operating systems are demanding projects. They touch every aspect of an organization.

At scale, an operating system offers reliable, consistent, reproducible management that is shared throughout an organization. When properly designed and calibrated, it is:

- **Reliable**: it's what creates the bonding with clients
- **Consistent**: its parts fit together to offer the same experience
- **Reproducible**: it produces the same results over and over
- **Shared**: it's used the same way throughout the organization

By nature, operating systems are designed for a specific context. When external challenges arise, or the distribution of knowledge changes, operating systems need to adapt. In the new business context, the operating system of most organizations needs an update if it was designed for traditional management. Traditional, control-based operating systems are no longer adequate in a dynamic environment where highly engaged people need to apply their full talent.

THE RISKS
OF DOING NOTHING

Digitalization and the changing nature of work are the two trends that fundamentally challenge traditional management systems and organizational structures. Thy represent a silent revolution where the normal – what we have all learned – does not work any more.

In the new, dynamic context:

- Managers can't tell people what to do
- Control is exercised by letting go of control
- Talent drives strategy
- Implementation requires small teams and tasks
- Complex systems must be scaled down
- Companies make money by not focusing on money

Current managerial operating systems and leaders, with 20th-century assumptions, are unsuited to handle these counterintuitive ideas. Digitalization and different work modes disrupt traditional operations. They're interferences. Businesses lose twofold as interferences reduce performance and unused knowledge limits the potential.

When work systems change, management systems need to follow. Even in a traditional, stable environment, the risks associated with not doing anything are high. The clues come from five myths detailed in 'Why Strategy Execution Unravels – and What to Do About It' (Sull, Homkes and Sull, 2015), an extensive study on implementation practices.

Myth 1: Implementation equals alignment. Managers use objectives, cascading objectives, measuring progress and rewarding performance as their traditional ways to align with strategy. When asked how they would improve implementation, they generally said with more of the same tools, such as 'management by objectives' and 'balanced scorecards.' And, most executives would argue that their organization is good at alignment. So why, then, are companies struggling with implementation?

When asked about commitments, 84% of managers say that they can rely on their bosses. But only 9% (Sull, Homkes and Sull, 2015) say they can rely on colleagues in other functions and units all the time. When managers cannot rely on colleagues in other parts of the organization, they duplicate efforts, let promises slip, delay deliverables or pass up attractive opportunities – all dysfunctional, damaging behaviours.

However, even in companies with effective practices for cascading objectives throughout their hierarchies, the systems and routines for horizontal coordination often lack teeth. Tools may be in place, but managers don't believe in them. Vertical dominates horizontal.

Myth 2: Implementation means sticking to the plan. For most managers, creating a strategy means establishing detailed plans that explain who should do what, by when, and with what resources. Strategic planning and budgeting have long been the backbone of strategy implementation. Deviations from plans are seen as a lack of discipline that undermines implementation.

Unfortunately, fixed plans don't survive any dynamic reality. Managers need to adapt to the facts on the ground and overcome unexpected obstacles in order to capture valuable opportunities. Adjustments to reality require agility.

The lack of agility is a major obstacle to strategy implementation in most companies. A third of executives admit to difficulties in adapting to changing circumstances. But most organizations react so slowly that they miss opportunities. Just as managers want more structure and processes for coordination, they want more of the same to adapt to changing circumstances and flexibility in the allocation of resources.

Myth 3: Communication equals understanding. Many managers believe that relentless communication on strategy is important. Most would agree that they're clear about top priorities. But, when asked to name the top priorities, few can name just two. Not only are strategic objectives poorly understood, but they often seem unrelated to one another or disconnected from strategy. Fewer than a third of senior managers understand the connection between corporate priorities. Among supervisors and team leaders, that percentage is even lower.

The amount of communications is not the issue, as 90% of managers believe (Sull, Homkes and Sull, 2015) that top leaders communicate frequently. How can so much communication lead to such a poor understanding? After all, the only thing that matters is what is being understood.

Myth 4: A performance culture drives implementation. When implementation fails, many managers point to a weak performance culture as the root cause. But implementation is rarely part of the official and explicit core values. However, it is an important part of the implicit culture when decisions need to be made on a day-to-day basis.

Past performance is the predominant factor when people decisions are made. But a culture that supports implementation must recognize other things as well, such as collaboration, agility and teamwork.

The excessive emphasis on performance can hinder implementation in a subtle way. When making performance goals is most important, managers start gaming their performance commitments, and the result is mediocrity.

The most critical issue with many corporate cultures is that they reward performance more than coordination and collaboration. When asked about that, most managers would agree that sacrificing collaboration in favour of performance is acceptable.

Myth 5: Implementation should be driven from the top. A strong emphasis on top leaders negotiating performance objectives with their subordinates, and monitoring their progress, might work in the short-term. It signals top-down implementation.

But most decisions in larger organizations are made at the client front, with leaders and employees who get the work done. Top-down management by objectives undermines what middle management and supervisors do in organizations. Delegated leadership shines.

Most middle managers live up the organization's values and goals most of the time. They do an especially good job reinforcing performance and holding teams accountable.

Many executives try to solve the problem of implementation – and with it, efficiency – by reducing complexity to one thing. They: tighten the alignment up and down the hierarchy; stick to plans or ignore them; communicate frequently but with little understanding; focus on goal achievement; and look to the top when making decisions. This creates a culture full of viruses that interfere with implementation and performance rather than unlock the potential. These myths are the hallmark of traditional management.

In 2000, Gallwey introduced a simple but powerful formula in *The Inner Game of Work*:

> **PERFORMANCE = POTENTIAL - INTERFERENCES**

Leaders who manage with an operating system designed for analogue when digital takes over face daily interferences. This impacts employees, too, with mounting interferences and missing performance. When people with knowledge cannot engage and apply their talent, their talent is unused, and the business misses out on performance. With an interference-free operating system, people can put their talent to work. Knowledge is a capability that grows with its use. Engaging that knowledge must be in the interest of leaders, the business and all other stakeholders.

The risks of 'business as usual' are substantial and can include lack of performance, unengaged people and missed opportunities. And this is regardless of whether businesses operate in a stable environment or a dynamic one. The solution is to have a managerial operating system without viruses, where people can unlock their talent to deliver sustainable performance – consistently, reliably and robustly – with agile features.

FOUR TENSIONS OF MANAGEMENT

The operating system for 21st-century management balances the tension between these risks and the potential. Employees want their leaders to distinguish between:

- Volatility and focus
- Uncertainty and energy
- Complexity and clarity
- Ambiguity and direction

Figure 3 illustrates these four tensions, with the challenges boxed in the centre and surrounded by four answers to those challenges.

Positive tensions exploit the potential. Negative tensions are interferences. Positive tensions are little talked about because when things are normal, there is no real concern. The negatives are a frequent outcome of classic employee surveys, reflected in such comments as: 'lack of information,' 'unclear strategy,' 'missing energy,' and 'lack of focus.' They get all the management attention.

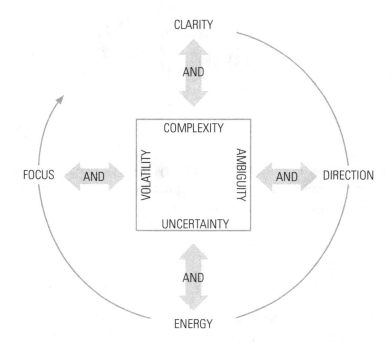

FIGURE 3: TENSIONS OF MANAGEMENT

COMPLEXITY AND CLARITY

For people in a context with increasing complexity, it is hard to see clearly and identify valuable opportunities. There is a tendency to simplify and try to reduce complexity.

Managers want to offer clarity and control. Traditional ways are to add bureaucracy, with routines and methodologies intended to reduce complexity. But knowledgeable employees can self-responsibly look for clarity to address complexity and the means to find purpose.

It's the negative tension between complexity and the need for clarity that creates interference, such as missing information, unclear tasks and lack of purpose. A dynamic operating system can balance these tensions. It relies on self-responsibility and people with a high degree of awareness to cope with complexity. They ask: What's my purpose?

AMBIGUITY AND DIRECTION

Ambiguity leaves a fuzzy future with many options. It's hard for people to select valuable opportunities, and there's an inherent risk of missing opportunities. Difficult decisions, to be sure.

Managers want to rely on their experience, and do it on their own. The traditional ways are to use power – to decide, guide and direct. But employees with knowledge want to apply their skills and know-how, and they want to take responsibility. They connect with other people to enhance knowledge.

The negative tension between ambiguity and the need for direction creates interferences. These can include hesitant management decisions, neglecting people skills and knowledge, and getting out of synch with strategy. Management just doesn't understand. A dynamic operating system relies on delegation, with sufficient choice and support for people to take risks and select the right opportunities. People ask: Who and what can I rely on?

UNCERTAINTY AND ENERGY

Uncertainty leads to hesitant action and limits the energy. It poses the risk of not turning opportunities into value, and prompts the ineffective use of resources.

Managers want to motivate, encourage and assign resources. The traditional way is by telling people what to do, and asking them to trust the decisions that are made from on high. But people are more likely to trust their own resources, and those around them, than something from management.

The negative tension between uncertainty and the ineffective use of resources creates interferences that can include mistrust, inaction and value destruction. Dynamic operating systems build on trust. They align resources by creating autonomous teams that collaborate. They ask: What support do I get?

VOLATILITY AND FOCUS

Volatility distracts attention. There's the risk of deviating from chosen paths and opportunities, and losing focus. Volatility requires constant refocusing of attention.

Managers want to (re)direct attention. The traditional way of doing this is with detailed targets. People have the ability to focus, so all they need is a attention.

Negative tension between volatility and focus creates interferences that can include changing goals, distractions and ineffective use of time. Dynamic operating systems support people to focus their attention. They ask: How do I stay on track?

THE PEOPLE-CENTRIC FOUNDATION

People-Centric Management (Figure 4) is about reconciling tensions between the challenges that people face and the opportunities they have to create value.

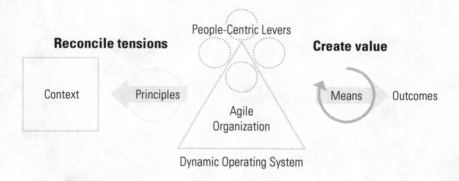

FIGURE 4: THE PEOPLE-CENTRIC FOUNDATION

Four levers determine people-centric at scale. Principles help people cope with the inner- and outer-challenges of their work. And the means ignite and channel the people's energy to deliver the expected outcomes. People-centric aligns with agile organization and demands and operating system with dynamic capabilities.

Reconciliation and value creation require that managers simultaneously 'work *on* the system' while they 'work *in* the system.' Work *in* the system is the day-to-day work of people-centric managers. Work *on* the system is the work of designing the operating system in support of management's work *in* the system.

People-centric refers to the mindset, the skill set and the tool-set needed to balance efficiency with innovation, to exploit and to explore, and to enable stability and cooperation – the features of an agile organization. People-centric levers establish that people-centric foundation.

JUST ANOTHER MANAGEMENT FAD?

Management is known for a high frequency of fads. For years, managers have been attracted to the latest tools, practices and incantations. Decision trees, zero-based budgeting, business process reengineering, balanced scorecards, Six Sigma and core competencies have all risen and fallen. There's been no drop-off in this trend chasing over the past decade or so, and there is more to come, for sure.

People-centric is different. It entails a deliberate and explicit shift in management that separates from the traditional, efficiency-driven focus of cost-cutting and bureaucracy to bring people, purpose, relationships and cooperation back into focus.

First, most growth firms adopt various forms of people-centric principles to support their development. Second, the power in the marketplace has shifted to the customer, who insists on instant, individual, incremental value. Most large bureaucracies can't deliver that. Third, top talent moves to where their skills are valued and where they can apply their gifts. They won't tolerate bureaucracy and mediocre management.

There is no alternative to people-centric. My observations are that while many leaders condemn bureaucracy, few claim successes in defeating it. Tactical victories to cut layers of management, trim head office staff or reengineer processes are generally small and quickly reversed. It's a fact that busting bureaucracy always seeds the need for more bureaucracy, and the desired trend is reversed. People-centric is here to stay. It's a defining feature of People-Centric Management.

Four levers offer choices between traditional and People-Centric Management. Four principles resolve the tensions that the environmental triggers pose. Four means enable people to create value and deliver the expected outcomes. The choice between traditional or people-centric must always be made with performance in mind.

Chapter 1 explains the 'why' of People-Centric Management. Chapters 2-8 describe 'what' capabilities are needed to enable it, while Chapters 9-11 offer the steps on 'how' to make it work. And then, Chapter 12 spells out the decisions that make people-centric your priority.

THE NEW BUSINESS CONTEXT

People-Centric Management with four principles is the means to succeed in the new business context.

KEY CHAPTER IDEAS

Changes in the external environment, and in the nature of work, trigger the shift to people-centric. People-centric beats traditional management in any context.

People-Centric Management requires balance in the set of four tensions:
* Complexity and clarity
* Ambiguity and direction
* Uncertainty and energy
* Volatility and focus

ACTION AGENDA

In the new context, leaders need to simultaneously work *on* the system while they work *in* the system.

FURTHER READING

Drucker, PF (1997). *Managing in a Time of Great Change.* Abingdon: Routledge..

Gallwey, WT (2000). *The Inner Game of Work.* New York: Random House.

Hamel, G (2006). The Why, What, and How of Management Innovation. *Harvard Business Review*, February.

Michel, L; Anzengruber, J; Wölfle, M; and Hixson, N (2018). Under What Conditions do Rules-Based and Capability-Based Management Modes Dominate? *Special Issue Risks in Financial and Real Estate Markets Journal*, 6(32).

Ulrich, D; and Smallwood, N (2004). Capitalizing on Capabilities. *Harvard Business Review*, June.

Wüthrich, HA; Osemtz, D; and Kaduk, S (2006). *Musterbrecher: Führung neu erleben* [Braking patterns, how leaders re-experience leadership]. Wiesbaden: Gabler.

CHAPTER

FOUR
PEOPLE-
CENTRIC
LEVERS

Now that we've provided some clarity on the new business context, in this chapter we will explore the people-centric framework (Figure 5) with principles, means and triggers. These levers will guide the choice between traditional and People-Centric Management with implications on the operating system.

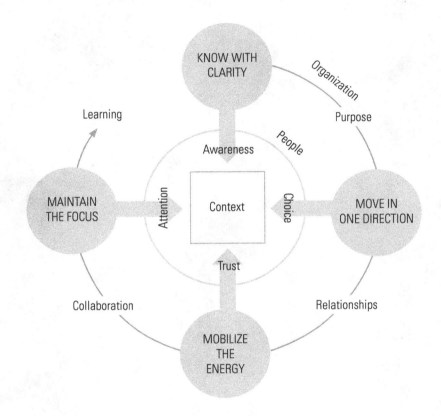

FIGURE 5: FOUR PEOPLE-CENTRIC LEVERS

We start in the centre of the diagram with the contextual triggers that articulate the outer game: the challenges people face when they do work. Next, we identify four inner-game principles that help people perform and simultaneously address their challenges. We then further explore the four means that put People-Centric Management into action: how people apply the inner game to address outer-game challenges. In combination, we describe the four management levers by contrasting traditional with people-centric.

In Chapter 1, The New Business Context, we explored the tensions between the external challenges and the demands on management and work. We referred to the need to establish an operating system that helps businesses successfully identify and extract value from opportunities. Context and the operating system take centre stage with the four people-centric levers.

INNER-GAME PRINCIPLES

We have already pointed to the clues to reconciling the tensions, the four principles of the inner game. People are best equipped to cope with and resolve these tensions by following four inner-game work principles:

- **Awareness** is the principle by which people cope with complexity
- **Choice** is the principle by which people handle ambiguity
- **Trust** is the principle by which people address uncertainty
- **Attention** is the principle by which people deal with volatility

The inner game is a mental technique developed by Timothy Gallwey (2000) that enables people to cope with the outer game – the challenges encountered when they perform work. Simultaneously, the inner game helps people learn and perform at their peak by applying their knowledge, skills, experience and talents. These four principles form the foundation for people-centric work.

THE MEANS OF WORK

People-centric work requires purpose (the ability to find meaning); relationships (the ability to connect and interact); collaboration (most work requires more than one person to complete the task); and learning (the ability to adapt to changing customer needs). Here's why these are so important:

- **Purpose** is the foundation for motivation and self-responsibility. People need answers to questions like, 'What is my purpose?' and 'How do I find meaning?'

- **Relationships** connect people. People need an answer to, 'Who can I rely on?'
- **Collaboration** coordinates the work of people. They need an answer to, 'What support do I get?'
- **Learning** refers to the ability to perform, innovate and grow. People need an answer to, 'How do I stay on track?'

In combination with the inner game, the four means function as the hidden driving force that creates value and delivers the outcomes. With this, the four people-centric levers guide the answers to these essential questions.

PEOPLE-CENTRIC LEVERS

The four people-centric levers offer a choice between traditional and People-Centric Management. They are:
- How do we know with clarity?
- How do we move in one direction?
- How do we mobilize the energy?
- How do we maintain the focus?

Traditional management favours bureaucracy, power, command and targets. People-centric, on the other hand, is about self-responsibility, self-organization, delegation and attention.

As you'll see in the following four graphics, people-centric levers offer sliders with a choice that spans two operating modes. While sliders offer a choice, they often have an ambidextrous capacity (O'Reilly and Tushman, 2004). The sliders may indicate simultaneous use of both, or a mix of the two. For example, agility needs stability. A well-functioning managerial system serves as a stable platform. Agile without a stable platform is like a spring – it only works as a spring when it's fixed on one end.

HOW DO WE KNOW WITH CLARITY?

Knowing with clarity identifies opportunities. It represents the capability to raise awareness, understand, and find purpose despite complexity. Lever 1 (Figure 6) identifies how we help people understand and find purpose between traditional command styles and people-centric through self-responsibility.

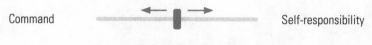

Command ———————————————— Self-responsibility

FIGURE 6: LEVER 1 – KNOW WITH CLARITY

In traditional command-oriented organizations, the goal is efficiency and reliability as the means to deliver shareholder value. Managers act as controllers and tell people what to do. In people-centric organizations, self-responsible teams delight their customers. With people-centric, the management task is to help people find purpose with customers first.

When knowledge is located with managers, command refers to the practice of them using information and routines to identify opportunities and offer direction. Command tends to increase complexity rather than supporting people's efforts to cope with it. Traditional management uses instruction for people to understand and follow direction. But purpose is found, not given. With distributed knowledge, people-centric promotes self-responsibility with people who are aware, and able to identify opportunities and find meaning in what they do.

Purpose defines the meaning people attach to what they do. Knowing with clarity helps people understand, filter opportunities and, ultimately, find purpose. With this, they're able to deal with complexity and create value for their customers.

HOW DO WE MOVE IN ONE DIRECTION?

To move in one direction is the ability to select valuable opportunities. Choice requires the alignment of forces and connecting people around purpose and direction, despite ambiguity. Lever 2 (Figure 7) identifies how people align to form teams between applying traditional power and dynamic delegation.

Power   Delegation

FIGURE 7: LEVER 2 – MOVE IN ONE DIRECTION

In traditional organizations, power sits with managers who have people reporting to them. The relationship is between the manager and the employee. With a dynamic operating system, responsibility is delegated to teams at the client front. The role of the manager now is to offer direction and a supportive work environment.

With knowledge concentrated at the top, managers use power to tell people what the direction is and what the expectations are in following it. Power limits the use of knowledge in selecting the right opportunities when dealing with an ambiguous context. Traditional management applies power by using rules that help managers select valuable opportunities. With distributed knowledge, managers use systems to delegate the decision-making to where the knowledge is. Choice helps people select valuable opportunities and identify the direction.

Relationships define how people connect and align with each other to increase their knowledge and access capabilities to get work done. People who move in one direction make meaningful choices. As such, they can cope with ambiguity and create value.

HOW DO WE MOBILIZE THE ENERGY?

Mobilizing the energy refers to how we turn opportunities into value. It is the capability to trust our own resources and those around us, and to get things done despite uncertainty. Lever 3 (Figure 8) identifies how we mobilize the energy to collaborate between traditional bureaucracy and self-organization.

Bureaucracy   Self-organization

FIGURE 8: LEVER 3 – MOBILIZE THE ENERGY

Bureaucracy reigns in traditional organizations, with work being coordinated by managers, rules and plans. With a dynamic operating system, self-organized teams coordinate and collaborate while being supported by people-centric leadership practices.

When knowledge is concentrated at the top, managers coordinate work through routines and by telling people what they should be doing. Bureaucracy pushes uncertainty aside rather than reducing it. Traditional management applies bureaucracy rather than trusting people. But, trust is the fastest management concept yet devised (Sprenger, 2007). Knowledgeable people trust their own capabilities to get work done. As such, agile promotes self-organization with motivated people who work in teams and turn opportunities into value.

Collaboration defines how people mobilize resources to coordinate work. Mobilizing the energy helps people bundle their efforts. In doing so, they can handle uncertainty and create value.

HOW DO WE MAINTAIN THE FOCUS?

Maintaining the focus is about sticking with the chosen opportunity. It's the capability to focus attention and learn despite volatility. Lever 4 (Figure 9) identifies how we focus and learn between traditional target setting and people-centric paying attention.

Targets   Attention

FIGURE 9: LEVER 4 – MAINTAIN THE FOCUS

Traditional organizations are preoccupied with tight performance targets and goal achievement for efficiency and reliability. People-centric teams use attention to maintain their focus on the customer, supported by transparency, learning, sharing and continuous improvement. Focus of attention is natural to people. It's people centric.

When knowledge is concentrated at the top, managers apply tools with narrow targets to ensure that people stay on track, don't get distracted and follow the chosen opportunity. Narrow targets function like detailed prescriptions and operating procedures. Targets cannot deal with volatility; they're always off. And so, people follow instructions, miss targets often and don't learn. With distributed knowledge, attention mobilizes the ability of people to constantly focus attention. Focus of attention is the clue to learning.

Learning refers to the means by which people pay attention, refocus when needed, and enhance knowledge to constantly learn and improve performance. With this, people cope with volatility and create value for their clients.

As a whole, people-centric comprises the following:

- Put customers first. In line with Drucker's thinking, the purpose of the firm is to create a customer.
- Carry out work in networks of small teams, with delegated responsibility and a focus on delivering value to customers.
- Remove bureaucracy. Enable self-organization, release the energy, and offer resources on demand to turn opportunities into value.
- Lead through attention, to maintain the focus and let go of control, opening the search for new opportunities.

Four levers offer a choice between traditional and people-centric. The shift from traditional to people-centric means a different way to work, organize and manage.

DISCUSSIONS OF PEOPLE-CENTRIC MANAGEMENT

The reality for most people inside many organizations is that work doesn't work. The ways businesses are managed and organized make it harder, rather than easier, for people to work. The way decisions are made slows things down when speed is essential. Traditional collaboration and communications make us feel like we'd be better off working by ourselves than working together.

Before getting into a detailed discussion of the People-Centric Management framework, it's helpful to remember important foundations, discuss current trends, share some concerns, suggest paths that should be omitted and establish the prerequisites in the space between traditional and people-centric.

FOUNDATIONS

Bureaucracy. The original idea to structure administrative work goes way back to the sociologist and political economist Max Weber (1928), with his renowned writings on modern bureaucracy. He argued that firms needed to get organized in order to capture business opportunities. Authority, control, division of labour, hierarchical structures, formal rules and human interactions were the themes. But Weber was also critical of unfettered bureaucracy, as it poses a threat to freedom through mounting rules and control. Today, the term bureaucracy often evokes Weber's concerns, as it keeps organizations from being flexible and fast, and forces them to follow command and control rules instead of being able to apply their talent. People-Centric Management suggests that bureaucracy is needed more than ever if businesses want to delight their customers, but that it has a different look and feel.

Limited Attention. The economist and political scientist Herbert A Simon (1957) defined what we now call 'limited attention.' He noted that when there's an abundance of information, attention becomes a scarce resource, since people cannot digest it all. Harvard Business School academics Robert Simons and Antonio Dávila (1998) extended the concept to what they call return on management: productive organizational energy released, divided by management time and attention invested. People-Centric Management is about making management more effective in a context where talent, skills and knowledge are more important than ever.

Levers of Control. Simons (1995), in his seminal book, *Levers of Control: How Managers use Innovative Control Systems to Drive Strategic Renewal*, expanded the concept of control. He included interactive control systems, diagnostic control systems, belief systems and boundary systems as the means for people to balance opportunities and attention. Levers of control provide an important foundation for People-Centric Management, by extending them to include a Leadership Scorecard and a Leadership Toolbox.

Beyond Budgeting. Strategic agility has its origins with finance experts Jeremy Hope and Robin Fraser (2003), in their book, *Beyond Budgeting: How Managers Can Break Free from the Annual Performance Trap*. They reframed the use of systems and tools in support of a dynamic business environment. The 12 'beyond budgeting' principles – values, governance, transparency, teams, trust, accountability, goals, rewards, planning, coordination, resources and self-controls – enable business agility. People-Centric Management applies beyond budgeting principles.

Management Models. The academic Julian Birkinshaw, in *Reinventing Management* (2010), suggests four management models – planning, quest, science and discover – in response to how companies coordinate activities, make and communicate decisions, set objectives and motivate employees. In doing so, he established the foundation for agile management. People-Centric Management offers that choice of models.

Dynamic Capabilities. Dynamic capabilities[6] are configurations of resources (talent, routines, rules, competencies, structures, etc.) that enable organizations to continuously adapt to rapid changes in the environment.[7] We'll define these as capabilities without negative interference from traditional change programmes. Agility is a specific dynamic capability. As such, People-Centric Management is deeply rooted in the theory of dynamic capabilities.

TRENDY ORGANIZATIONAL MODELS

People-centric is a core element of various organizational models that promote employee engagement, innovation and collectiveness rather than bureaucracy and self-driven models. Here is a selection of such models:

Holacracy. Introduced in 2007 by management coach Brian J Robertson (2015), the model replaces traditional hierarchies with a 'peer-to-peer' operating system that claims to increase transparency, accountability and agility. The idea is to distribute authority to teams, and empower people to take executive roles and make meaningful decisions. People-Centric Management promotes decentralized management with empowered teams. However, it does so without adding bureaucracy, without another top-down programme and without replacing hierarchy.

Responsive Organizations. These are built to learn and rapidly respond through an open flow of information, encouraging experimentation and learning through rapid cycles. This is an organization that focuses on networks of employees, customers and partners, and is motivated by a shared purpose. People-Centric Management encourages learning and networks but does not promote experimentation, as one does not experiment with people.

Sociocracy. This was first conventionalized as a model by philosopher Auguste Comte in the 19th century and is now known as Sociocracy 3.0. It describes companies and teams that collaborate as self-managed, and where everyone gets a democratic voice. Its design is to grow an effective, agile and resilient organization. People-Centric Management is designed to enable collaboration and self-organization, but I stop short of viewing corporations as democracies.

Teal. Reintroduced by corporate coach Frederic Laloux (2014) in his book, *Reinventing Organizations,* the concept of 'teal' is based on spiral dynamics elements (Graves, 1970). The idea is that peer relationships and self-management with agile capabilities focus less on the bottom-line and shareholder value, through a strong evolutionary purpose. People-Centric Management emphasizes purpose as a means of motivation. And, it encourages simultaneous intangible and tangible value creation.

New organizational models grow like mushrooms. Their proponents always find an example where it worked in practice. That's the point. These models have been designed to fit the specifics of that organization. This does not mean that one can simply copy and paste what has proven successful in one place to make it work somewhere else.

CONCERNING ISSUES

Management or leadership. The conversation goes on, and thousands of articles are written every year about the difference. For me, leadership is fundamentally about people. Management deals with resources, buildings, IT systems and all other inanimate things. In practical terms, separating people leadership from day-to-day management of the business is a good practice, to deal with a dynamic context and embrace agility. That's what People-Centric Management is all about.

Digital. Today, 'digital' is used as an attribute for just about everything: work, business, leadership, management, organization and more. It implies modern, better and *the future*. People-Centric Management looks at digitalization as a technology that enables people to do meaningful work. It changes the way we work, manage and lead people.

New work. It's in fashion. Just about everybody writes about it and has an opinion. That's when I stop reading. Flexible and remote work, digital skills, collaboration, customer-focus, fast decision-making and future-oriented task are attributes cited with 'new work.' Most are not new, and not widely researched in scientific management literature. People-Centric Management implies new work, and is specific on its implications for organization, management and leadership.

Employee engagement. The Gallup analytics organization tells us that 87% (Gallup, 2020) of employees globally are disengaged at work. It's no surprise. If efficiency, repeatability and scalability dominate – but managers hire diverse, talented individuals with new skill sets, and ask them to do the same job, follow the same metrics, and conform to drive productivity through incentives and punishment – you get disengagement and mediocrity. People would have to break rules to do something extraordinary. Regardless of what managers say, people feel isolated, standardized and uninformed. The disappointment about employee engagement initiatives aimed at well-being and new work is that they invariably fail unless the meaning of work is being addressed. People-Centric Management is about putting meaning back into work.

Ecosystems. The talk about ecosystems is in fashion, but it's not new. Business ecosystems are groups of companies, platform providers, government agencies, independent contractors, co-creating customers and others whose contributions come together to create value. This is a trend that demands agile capabilities from its parts: small entrepreneurial teams dominate, and leaders become influencers with the ability to build communities and inspire alignment. Nothing new there. Ecosystems have long been part of management thinking and practices, especially with SMEs in Europe. What is new is that technologies enable networking and collaboration in ways we haven't had in the past. This trend will change large organizations. Federal structures and agile management combine to accelerate the change. People-Centric Management starts with the team, expands to the organization, and extends to ecosystems. The principles and practices remain the same.

Bashing on the old. It's fashionable to rebuke top-down management and bureaucratic processes. The popular leadership literature is full of it. Old is bad, while new is great. But it's good practice to first work out what principles and processes are good for the stable functioning and consistency of an organization before getting rid of the old stuff. Sometimes, organizations throw out all the good stuff when they get rid of the old stuff. People-Centric Management will help you do a thoughtful 'spring cleaning' that preserves stability while enhancing agility.

Agile mindset. I cannot hear this any more. It's often lauded as being the solution to becoming nimble and agile. Simultaneously, it means a mindset that is less formal, less rules-driven, more productive and more creative. One should simply encourage people to speak up and provide feedback, quickly adapt to meet changing customer needs, and maintain a healthy work-life balance. I've learned from many projects that such recipes and principles don't deliver the kind of capability development and culture change that organizations must pursue to fulfil these demands. Agile requires much more than a mindset shift to translate into People-Centric Management. Agile mindset is great, but the difference comes with the complete agile toolset, mindset and skill set.

The 70% Change-Failure Myth. "50-70% of organizations that undertake a reengineering effort do not achieve the dramatic results they intended." (Hammer and Champy, 1993). Since that historic statement, supported by change management guru John P Kotter (Kotter, 1996), many other prominent writers and consultants have kept quoting these numbers with little reflection on where the data is coming from and how far back it dates. It's time to challenge that myth. Change management has grown over the past 30 years to become the management tool and approach to help companies make changes in their business. The challenge comes from the fact that change management has been used as a fix for all sorts of problems. It delivers what it promises: change. Also, many users fail to recognize that contexts may have changed during the ongoing change, so they keep changing in a dynamic world. People-Centric Management builds on speed, agile and resilient capabilities, which belong to the category of dynamic capabilities. They're capabilities that help organizations permanently establish the capacity to anticipate and adapt to changes as they happen in the environment. Change approaches and tools become part of everyday managerial practices. It's now a practice that does not drain the energy of those involved. These capabilities establish a context where people can unlock their full talent and potential.

PATHS THAT LEAD ASTRAY

'Error Culture.' Where does this nonsense come from? Whenever things go wrong in Europe, we call for the right 'error culture.' There is no such thing as an error culture, but there is a demand to learn from errors. There is no creative and efficient organization that runs without errors. This means that dealing with errors is part of every leader's day-to-day work. Simply put, if you reprimand for errors, your team may indeed follow every rule, but they'll refrain from taking any risks. As a result, your organization will deliver average performance. Is that what you want? The agile way is simple: accept that errors happen, learn from them without blaming, and ensure that they don't happen twice. People-Centric Management takes the fear out of operations.

Motivation. The literature is full of how leaders need to motivate their people. All of these ideas are driven by one notion that stems from an antiquated assumption about people: they need to be motivated to get things done. Let me set this straight, and I get prominent support for this: "Leaders can only demotivate. People are motivated by definition." (Sprenger, 2010). Motivation stems from self-responsibility and purpose. The ability to say 'no' drives self-responsible work, which is by definition the foundation of any motivation. So, please, leaders, stop *motivating* your people. People-Centric Management suggests purpose and self-responsibility if you want to be agile and nimble.

Fear. If you are a leader who searches for errors and missteps by your people, then you're likely leading by fear. There is no work without faults. Mistakes happen. Today's dynamic environment demands that people take risks and try new things. So, if you want to kill any creativity and innovation, keep leading by fear. And, perhaps, *People-Centric Management* is the wrong book for you.

PREREQUISITES

Federalism. The focus of this book is on agile management more than organizational constructs. However, I'm making an assumption on structures, and that is that there's merit in the concept of federalism. In short, humans work best in small groups, where there is trust and where one can make a difference. But, the reality is that most corporate organizations employ thousands of people. The sheer size of these companies makes it hard to find purpose, build relationships, collaborate and learn as a means to grow. As a Swiss citizen, I favour the federal principle. That's the structure by which Switzerland is governed. Federalism is the opposite of centralization, and it is governed by the principle of subsidiarity. This means that the power is with the smallest unit, which then delegates to the centre only things that the centre can do better for all of them. Agile assumes that kind of structure. It's the small unit that allows the whole to grow.

Talent. Talent selection is crucial, and it's important to be rigorous about it. Talent selection is usually one of the weak points in any agile organization. It is not sufficient to look at one-year performance or trust so called scientific selection factors. Developing good leaders is primarily a managerial job. Good leaders look for potential, and it's their responsibility to select and develop *their* leaders. In that sense, agile is not different from traditional. But in an agile organization, faulty leaders are more visible. People-Centric Management assumes that you get this right.

Teamwork. Agile builds on teamwork, self-responsibility and self-organization. They are the foundation of good teamwork. Agile amplifies the need for leaders to assemble teams that can shoulder responsibility. In teams, people need to complement each other. Therefore, you mustn't let your leaders pick their own teams – what you end up with is an inner circle around the boss. Simultaneously, you created a sort of disempowerment for those who are not in the inner circle. That creates toxic organizations. I know this is not what's done in most organizations, but experience has taught me the hard way. People-Centric Management demands that you care about the composition of your team.

Experience. It's often said that agile requires new leadership. Well, that's not truly new, and it has little to do with agile. Experience is important in most managerial contexts. People-Centric Management is not naive. A successful people-centric shift requires experience from those who have done it before.

Values and standards. There is much discussion about values. But values without standards are like talk without action. It is important to understand what values look like in practice. That's what standards do. People-Centric Management with the Leadership Scorecard offers questions that will help you get standards right. But, there are two factors you'll need to keep in mind:

1. **It takes time.** Agile is about small teams that take on responsibility and get things done. That requires trust, and trust takes time. The People-Centric Management transformation is an evolution, not another top-down project.
2. **Partial fixes don't stick.** In agile organizations, the customer reigns. This is in contrast to traditional organizations where the manager is the boss and making money is the goal. There is an inherent tension between agile and management. In agile, making money is the result, not the goal. If, as a leader, you assume agile, you will face traditional throughout the organization. It's a conflict you cannot win. People-Centric Management promotes a shift in the entire organization.

This list of people-centric prerequisites is by no means complete. But, this introduction summarizes the main trends and issues I've observed over the years when organizations embark on people-centric initiatives.

The most exciting management and organization breakthroughs of the 21st century will not occur because of digitalization, but due to the expanding mindset of what the revolution means to being human.

PEOPLE-CENTRIC

Identifying people-centric with four people-centric levers is the key to greater impact when things change.

KEY CHAPTER IDEAS

People-centric consists of the set of four levers needed for innovation and business growth in a dynamic environment. It refers to four choices on how to find purpose, build relationships, collaborate and learn. As a prerequisite for applying these levers, the trigger, principles and means must be identified:

Triggers	Principles	Levers	Means
Complexity	Awareness	Know with clarity	Purpose
Ambiguity	Choice	Move in one direction	Relationships
Uncertainty	Trust	Mobilize the energy	Collaboration
Volatility	Attention	Maintain the focus	Learning

ACTION AGENDA

In preparation for People-Centric Management, clarify the following:
- What is the context your organization faces? How do you cope with that context? How do you help people perform despite that context?
- What is the distribution of knowledge in your organization? How do you enable people to apply their potential, knowledge and skills?

FURTHER READING

Michel, L (2013). The Performance Triangle: A Diagnostic Tool to Help Leaders Translate Knowledge into Action. *Organizational Cultures: An International Journal,* 12(2).

Nold, H; and Michel, L (2016). The Performance Triangle: A Model for Corporate Agility. *Leadership & Organizational Development Journal,* 37(3).

CHAPTER

KNOW
WITH
CLARITY

Imagine that you and your team have to make a decision in a complex, high-stakes situation with insufficient information. It's hard to see clearly – a frequent managerial problem. When complexity arises, there is no one way to solve the problem.

People-Centric Management suggests awareness as the principle to guide people in dealing with complexity, while purpose is the means to find meaning in what they do. Knowing with clarity (Figure 10) offers the people-centric solution for organizations to scale how people individually identify valuable opportunities despite complexity.

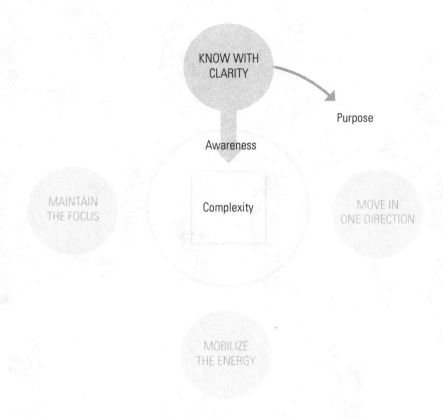

FIGURE 10: FOUR PEOPLE-CENTRIC LEVERS

Chapter 3 offers the principles, means and systems to resolve the 'clarity' tension by asking:

- How do we know with clarity?
- How do we identify opportunities despite complexity?
- How to reconcile tension between complexity and clarity?
- How do we enable people to find purpose?

The solution comes with a deep understanding of awareness, how people *understand*, and what they need to know with clarity. Having said that, we will explore options for how managers can help people find purpose. Then, we'll identify and determine the use of information tools to facilitate a shared understanding at scale, throughout an organization.

Complexity makes the search for valuable opportunities more difficult. People-centric puts clients first. Knowing with clarity ensures that people identify those opportunities that benefit clients through value creation, and it ultimately benefits all other stakeholders, despite that higher complexity.

CREATE
AWARENESS

How do we know with clarity? Awareness enables people to understand and engage with a deep sense of purpose. It is the key to managing in a complex environment.

Awareness is sensing by translating observed data into information without making a judgment about it. It is about having a clear understanding of the present. Non-judgmental awareness is the best way to sense what's going on. However, the more signals people receive, the more immune they become to the messages these signals contain.

Here is the test:

- Are people aware of what is happening around them?
- Can people sense minute changes in the work environment, internally or external to the organization?

ALTERNATIVES TO KNOW WITH CLARITY

How can you reconcile the tension between complexity and clarity? Lever 1 (Figure 11) offers traditional command and control, versus people-centric self-responsibility, as a choice based on where the knowledge resides. It's a choice of principles for a dynamic operating system to reconcile the tensions. The sliders suggest a choice as a mix between command and self-responsibility.

Distributed knowledge engaging people

Command ←|→ Self-responsibility

Concentrated knowledge and managerial control

Command ←|→ Self-responsibility

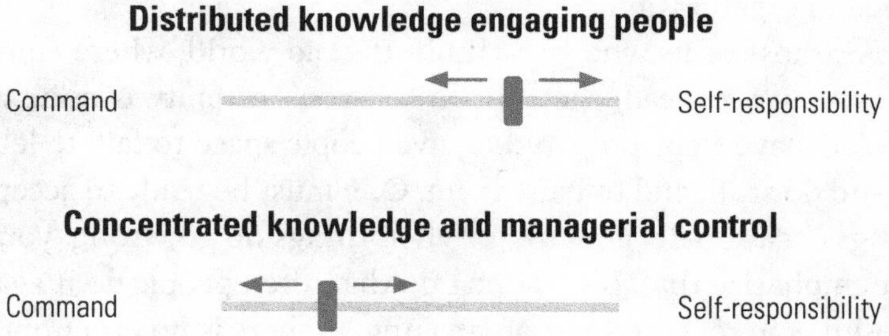

FIGURE 11: CHOICES FOR HOW TO KNOW WITH CLARITY

Moving the slider to the left: energy and decisions reside with managers who control what is being done and control the activities of their employees. Control assumes an image of mankind where people need be told what to do and purpose is provided.

Instructions are a means of explaining to people what to do. It is simply another word for command. Strict rules ensure that people do exactly what they've been told to do, and don't get distracted. Strict control ensures that they maintain their performance and achieve their goals. Once there, they require new, more challenging goals to restart their cycle of planning and implementation.

Moving the slider to the right: motivation relies on people who decide and act based on a deep sense of purpose, and meaning is achieved.

The responsibility theory assumes that people are self-motivated and want to get things done. This means providing them with observation points to focus their attention. Higher awareness means they sense early signs and have a significant degree of freedom to react to them. Choice is the foundation for responsibility.

Consider the purpose-versus-command dichotomy. In the old world, leaders documented in detail what they wanted people to do – employees were given tasks that fit within their job descriptions. Today's knowledge work is not a set of tasks because, in a dynamic situation, people should revert to purpose rather than being task-driven. Purpose helps them deal with the situation rather than simply following the process or waiting to be told what to do. Purpose is inherent in self-responsible action. Self-responsibility is the key to speed in organizations.

For most of us who grew up in the old world, where command was the way to lead, the shift to self-responsibility is quite a step. Leaders have to be prepared to give people space to fail, to let them go and do stuff, and to trust them. One must be ready to accept that things occasionally go wrong. When things do go wrong, you must not emphasize that. If you don't do that, then people do it again. As a result, you revert to micromanaging, as there is no other option.

FIND PURPOSE: MEANINGFUL WORK

What we often hear when the climate changes is something like, 'When we lost sight of the purpose in our work, we started a discussion on motivation.' When people experience their work as meaningful, they contribute with greater energy, and they're physically, mentally and emotionally fully present.

Purpose is created individually, subjectively. It is always 'me' that provides meaning to the world. In the words of philosopher and sociologist Jürgen Habermas, 1988, "There is no administrative production of purpose." It is called sense-making, not sense-giving. Purpose cannot be delivered. It needs to be found or produced individually.

As a leader and an employee, ask yourself:
- Do people have a strong shared sense of higher purpose?
- Does the purpose that motivates people inspire them to go above and beyond the minimum expectations?
- What is the impact my organization has on customers and society?
- How am I uniquely contributing to that purpose?

Individuals search for purpose. But, in tough times, purpose needs reinforcement. Agile techniques enable purpose at scale.

THE OPERATING SYSTEM TO UNDERSTAND

How do we enable people to find purpose? Information and immediate feedback raise awareness of what is important. This helps people understand what matters and focuses attention. Superior understanding requires that sensors are not on mute and amplifiers work properly.

Information and feedback mechanisms tie every organizational unit and employee to the umbrella firm. For example, performance information is reported to the centre as part of the individual accountability of employees, whereas directional feedback information moves to the periphery of an organization, where it is the duty of a manager to inform employees about strategy.

The operating system to understand (Figure 12) enables people to know what's going on. With this, leaders can help them make sense and answer 'What does that mean?' by translating data into meaning. Sense-making (Weick, 1995) is the technique they use. At scale, culture answers the question, 'What is our shared understanding?'

Information	**Command**	**Self-responsibility**
Context	Knowledge at the top	Complexity, distributed knowledge
Systems	Executive information, extensive performance measurement	Diagnostic information, few metrics, instant feedback
Leadership	Rigorous routines to tell people what to do	Interactive sense-making
Culture	Individual awareness, executive control	Collective awareness, shared understanding

FIGURE 12: THE OPERATING SYSTEM TO UNDERSTAND

Traditional information systems for command and control assume that knowledge is at the top. Executive information systems ensure that decisions are made based on data. Detailed performance information offers feedback for corrective action. Rigorous performance routines ensure that people know what to do. The result is a culture based on executive control.

BHAGs – the 'big, hairy, audacious goals' promoted by management gurus Jim Collins and Jerry Porras as the bold strategic vision statements with powerful, emotional appeal – are means to infuse work with meaning. Such goals are often articulated in a way that connects with people's values. In some organizations, these statements are so grandiose or unattainable that they contain little relevance or meaning for those who do the work. The result is a meaningless vacuum that creates cynicism and eventually impacts the reputation of leaders.

FIGURE 13: INFORMATION SYSTEMS

Dynamic information systems (Figure 13) support self-responsible people with knowledge that's distributed throughout the organization. Information works diagnostically. Few metrics offer feedback to where the work is being done. Leaders focus on interactions and offer sense-making. Collective awareness creates a culture with a shared understanding and purpose at its roots.

People-centric principles, agile means and dynamic operating systems resolve the tension between complexity and clarity. The solution comes from helping people at work understand with clarity and raise awareness of what matters. Purpose is the food for self-responsible people. With a sense of purpose, they search for opportunities despite the complexity of work.

LEVER 1: KNOW WITH CLARITY

Awareness is the means for people to address complexity. Simultaneously, awareness enables purpose.

KEY CHAPTER IDEAS

- Complexity cannot be reduced. People can only cope with it.
- Awareness to understand is the means for people to address complexity.
- At scale, organizations need to offer means to find purpose.
- The information system helps people understand and know with clarity.

ACTION AGENDA

Determine information capabilities and systems for clarity and purpose:

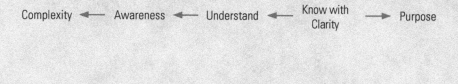

- Understand the degree of complexity and nature of knowledge.
- Decide on the principle of knowing with clarity to fit your context.
- Engage agile techniques that offer purpose.
- Identify the operating system for better understanding and to raise awareness.

FURTHER READING

Weick, K (1995). *Sensemaking in Organizations.* Thousand Oaks: Sage.

Sprenger, RK (2007). *Das Prinzip Selbstverantwortung: Wege zur Motivation* [The Self-Responsibility Principle: Paths to Motivation]. Frankfurt/New York: Campus.

Heywood S; and Turnball, D (2007). Cracking the Complexity Code. *McKinsey Quarterly*, 2.

CHAPTER

MOVE
IN ONE
DIRECTION

Think about what you would do with an important business decision when there are multiple future scenarios with similar probable outcomes. It's hard to make that decision. Think about how your people make decisions in a similar context. You and your people may need some principles to guide how you go about that decision-making.

People-Centric Management suggests a choice of two principles for dealing with ambiguity, and the means to build relationships and enhance knowledge. Moving in one direction (Figure 14) offers the people-centric solution for organizations to scale how people individually select valuable opportunities, despite ambiguity.

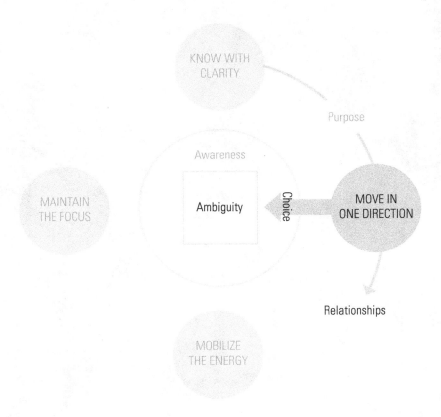

FIGURE 14: MOVE IN ONE DIRECTION

This chapter offers the principles, means and systems to resolve the 'direction' tension, including:

- How do we move in one direction?
- How do we select valuable opportunities despite ambiguity?
- How do we reconcile the tension between ambiguity and direction?
- How do we enable people to build relationships and enhance knowledge?

The solution comes from accepting choice, how people are supported in their *thinking* to assume responsibility, and what they need to move in one direction. It expands on the options of how managers can help people build relationships and enhance knowledge. Then, we explore how the strategy system can facilitate the thinking at scale in the organization.

In an ambiguous market environment, making a decision on a valuable business opportunity is a challenge. Dynamic means guiding the decision-making without limiting choice.

PROVIDE CHOICE

How do we move in one direction? Choice is the prerequisite for self-responsibility. But, direction and choice do not naturally correspond. Self-responsibility is the choice to take charge and move in the desired direction.

Choice means self-determination, whereas rules are determined from the outside. In an ambiguous context, people need choice. Here is the test:

- Are people empowered to use their creativity and make choices to effectively respond to customers, clients or other people inside and outside of the organization?
- Do people have freedom of action in line with the strategy?

ALTERNATIVES TO MOVE IN ONE DIRECTION

How do we reconcile the tension between ambiguity and direction? Lever 2 (Figure 15) offers traditional power mechanisms and people-centric delegation as the alternatives, based on the degree of ambiguity. The latter requires a dynamic operating system to reconcile the tensions. The sliders in Figure 15 offer a span between power and delegation.

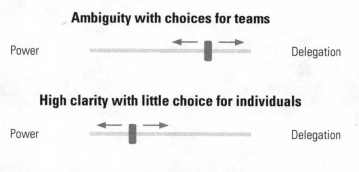

FIGURE 15: ALTERNATIVE FOR HOW TO MOVE IN ONE DIRECTION

Moving the slider to the left means exercising power. It refers to managers taking charge of key decisions that are then handed over to people for implementation. As such, power separates the thinking from the doing. Decisions are made at the top. The doing is with the rest of the organization. Power has worked well in context, with little change and highly repetitive tasks.

Power and hierarchy are two of the oldest principles of management. Hierarchy provides managers with the power and accountability to make decisions. It assumes that managers possess greater experience and superior wisdom. However, direction does not fare all that well in hierarchical settings.

Moving the slider to the right means delegation. Delegated responsibility helps organizations capture new challenges and innovate in an ambiguous context. For this to work, delegation needs choice based on principles rather than detailed standard operating procedures.

Collective wisdom uses the brains of many to make decisions. However, it's important to note the difference between opinions and decisions. Crowds may have opinions, but decision-making requires accountability for decisions. Collective decision-making is popular and has potential, but it has its disadvantages. Crowds are good at providing input for structured decisions but cannot be held accountable.

The use of collective wisdom requires a significant shift of mindset for many experienced managers in today's organizations. Delegation increases overall resilience in an ambiguous context.

CONNECT AND CULTIVATE RELATIONSHIPS

Relationships are an important means for addressing the challenges in an ambiguous context. Connected people with diverse knowledge make better decisions in any context, and with a variety of outcomes, than one lonely manager might.

Relationships are the cornerstone of every business transaction. In individualized people-to-people businesses, trust and agreement between employees and the organization are as important as relationships with external stakeholders. 'Relationship capital' counts as the essential value of a firm. But good relationships come at a price. They impose a challenge on every leader. Relationships also refer to connectivity. The greater the number of connections among people in an organization, the more restrictions and boundaries they place on one another. This limits their freedom of movement and their ability to perform (Stacey, 2000). This means relationships and connectivity must be tuned to an optimum level.

As a leader and employee, ask yourself:
- Do people have healthy relationships that build trust and agreement among employees and external stakeholders alike?
- Do the relationships among employees and stakeholders facilitate knowledge sharing and growth?
- How do I make it easier for employees to connect with their colleagues?
- How do I deepen relationships to build social glue?

Individuals connect and build relationships. Agile techniques enable relationships at scale.

THE OPERATING SYSTEM TO THINK

How do we enable people to build relationships and enhance knowledge? Knowledge people have a set of mental maps that help them make sense of situations and make decisions. The benefits for an organization come not only from individual thinking, but also from collective thinking. The thinking requires an opportunity to create meaning and asks for a deliberate choice to move in one direction.

The operating system to think (Figure 16) provides choice and direction to enable self-responsible people to move in one direction, and to align their work with the overall direction, as well as with each other. Agile strategy development is also an important feedback mechanism within the organization if leaders inform people about the strategy with their insights. An agile strategy leads to a shared intent at scale.

Strategy	**Power**	**Delegation**
Context	Clarity	Ambiguity
Systems	Executive retreat, planning as a strategy process, separated from implementation	Strategy as an integrated thought and action model, a creative learning process for every team
Leadership	One-directional messaging	Interactive strategy conversations
Culture	Choice restricted to executives, executive decisions, individual intent	Team contributions, shared intent

FIGURE 16: THE OPERATING SYSTEM TO THINK

Traditional strategy operating systems support executive thinking in contexts with high clarity. Executive retreats for strategy and planning are used to set direction. Leaders then communicate that direction throughout the organization. The result is a culture based on executive control and power through hierarchy.

Strategy requires stability. The move in one direction assumes that it remains stable for some time. But strategies and initiatives are abandoned so frequently that they appear to show a lack of attention. Not allowing sufficient time prevents employees from being able to adapt and align. It's awfully difficult for people to know where the organization's heading when things keep changing.

Dynamic strategy systems (Figure 17) enable thinking in ambiguous contexts. Strategy and implementation are part of a continuous learning process. Leaders interact and offer strategic insights. In combination, this creates a culture based on a shared intent for a delegated way of connected thinking.

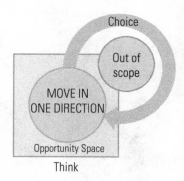

FIGURE 17: STRATEGY SYSTEMS

People-centric principles, agile means and dynamic systems resolve the tension between ambiguity and need for direction. The solution comes from providing choice to people with delegated responsibility. Relationships connect people with knowledge for aligned decisions on valuable opportunities in an ambiguous context.

LEVER 2: MOVE IN ONE DIRECTION

Choice is the means to cope with ambiguity. Simultaneously, choice determines relationships.

KEY CHAPTER IDEAS

- Ambiguity requires choice. Without choice, one cannot say no.
- Choice in thinking is the means for people to address ambiguity.
- At scale, organizations need to provide the means to build relationships.
- The operating system to think helps people move in one direction.

ACTION AGENDA

Determine thinking capabilities and systems for direction and relationship building:

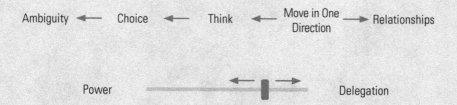

- Understand the degree of ambiguity and need for choice.
- Decide on the principle of 'move in one direction' that fits your context.
- Engage agile techniques for high connectivity.
- Identify the operating system for choice and to enhance relationships.

FURTHER READING

Von Krogh, G; Ichijo, K; and Nonaka, I (2000). *Enabling Knowledge Creation – How to Unlock the Mystery of Tacit Knowledge and Release the Power of Innovation.* Oxford: University Press.

Beer, M; and Eisenstat, RA (2004). How to Have an Honest Conversation About Your Business Strategy. *Harvard Business Review*, February.

CHAPTER

MOBILIZE THE ENERGY

You and your people are clear about what needs to get done and how to move in one direction. Now, let's look at bundling that energy to remove any uncertainty, and turning a valuable opportunity into the value you want to see.

People-Centric Management suggests trust as the principle for people to deal with uncertainty and the means to collaborate. Mobilizing the energy (Figure 18) is about how to scale people individually, turning valuable opportunities into value despite uncertainty.

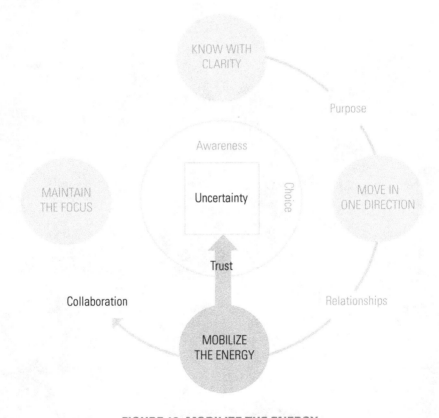

FIGURE 18: MOBILIZE THE ENERGY

This chapter offers the principles, means and systems to resolve the 'energy' tension. It addresses these questions:

- How do we mobilize energy and resources?
- How do we turn valuable opportunities into value, despite uncertainty?
- How do we reconcile the tension between uncertainty and energy?
- How do we enable people to collaborate?

The solution comes through building trust, providing the support people need to act, and delivering the resources they need to get things done. As such, we explore the options for how managers can help people collaborate. Then, we identify and suggest implementation systems that bundle energies at scale throughout the organization.

Uncertainty makes it difficult to turn opportunities into value. Risks are everywhere. People-centric builds on trust. Mobilizing the energy ensures that people are trusted and that there's trust in the capabilities of collaborators to overcome uncertainties and capture the value.

OFFER YOUR TRUST

How do we mobilize energy? Trust is a prerequisite for self-organization. Leaders must have trust in teams that organize themselves. And, teams must trust their own capabilities in an uncertain context. Trust is the only feature to cope with high uncertainty.

Trust means speed and agility. It's the fastest management concept ever invented and the foundation for every business transaction. With trust, there's no need for any re-negotiation of contracts when things change. Managers choose between trust and mistrust, or responsibility and outside control. But, trust must be earned. The best way to earn trust is by delivering on promises.

Here is the test:

- Do people view management as credible, fair and respectful of the needs, concerns and conditions of employees?
- Do people have the self-efficacy and confidence to trust in their own decisions and actions?

ALTERNATIVES TO MOBILIZING THE ENERGY

How do we reconcile the tension between uncertainty and energy? Lever 3 separates people-centric self-organization from traditional bureaucracy as the alternative when trust is needed in an uncertain context. It's the choice of the people-centric principle, with dynamic implementation systems that reconcile the tensions. The sliders in Figure 19 offer bureaucracy or self-organization as the alternatives to mobilizing the energy.

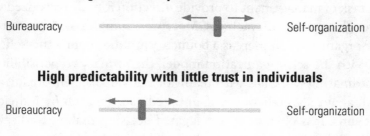

High uncertainty with trust in teams

Bureaucracy   Self-organization

High predictability with little trust in individuals

Bureaucracy   Self-organization

FIGURE 19: ALTERNATIVES TO MOBILIZING THE ENERGY

Moving the slider to the left increases bureaucracy. Bureaucracy refers to predetermined administrative procedures designed to get work done. It works well in a stable environment with standardized jobs that never change.

Bureaucracy places the responsibility for coordinating work into the hands of leaders and central staff. Even though bureaucracy has become a synonym for bad management, nobody would disagree with the need for efficiency through disciplined control, rigorous processes, clear rules and simple coordination.

The problem with bureaucracy is that it takes individuality and flexibility out of operations. This is especially challenging in a knowledge-driven work environment where creativity is required. It's important to note that bureaucracies that force people to adhere to a set of principles, or provide them with a set of methodologies and tools for consistent services, are needed in every organization. The challenge with bureaucracy is less its existence than its interpretation by managers.

Moving the slider to the right increases self-organization. Self-organization refers to individuals and teams that organize their own way of getting things done.

Physicist Hermann Haken's (1982) theory of the collaboration of elements within complex structures and dynamic systems states that collaboration and self-organization require constant outside energy. This means leaders should constantly invest time and attention in making self-organization and coordination work effectively in organizations. Self-organizing is not the same as self-directing. It is the task of management to provide direction for self-organized work through ongoing interactions. Moreover, complex systems can only self-organize when there is a boundary around them – the 'self.'

With the self-organization model, the primary responsibility for coordinating work lies with teams or individuals. Self-organization is all about spontaneous, self-initiated coordination by individuals or teams. It is obvious that delegated decision-making and self-organization go hand-in-hand. They enable agile and fast responses to challenges in a dynamic environment. A prerequisite for self-organization is guidance and structures that enable individuals to coordinate work without being distracted in all directions. Self-organization is not about letting things go or losing control.

NATURALLY COLLABORATE

Collaboration is an important means to address the challenge of an uncertain environment. Collective knowledge and many diverse minds are better than individuals at dealing with uncertainty.

Collaboration is an issue because of the complexity that increases with size. We keep adding functions, geographies, departments, services, client groups and other structures to our organizations. In a complex and networked world, where knowledge matters, collaboration is more important than ever. Every vertical structure creates barriers between people who need to work together, such as limited or distorted information flows. In addition, the fundamental cooperation problem of employees and organizations having different, and often conflicting, goals must be resolved. Vertical always dominates horizontal.

As a leader and employee, ask yourself:
- Do employees and stakeholders share unique knowledge and work together towards common goals, to achieve success in their everyday activities?
- Do people demonstrate trust, creativity and patience when working together as unexpected events occur?
- How do I encourage people to connect and collaborate?
- Who are the people I need to cooperate with to get work done? Where do I get support in that endeavour?

Individuals naturally collaborate. Engage agile techniques to develop self-organization at scale in organizations.

THE OPERATING SYSTEM TO ACT

How do we enable people to collaborate? Implementation systems facilitate the allocation, coordination and engagement of people to support others, and get support from each other to get work done. That requires trust.

The task is to mobilize the collective energy to get things done. People put their energy into things they care about. And, energy requires actions to be meaningful. Action requires the opportunity to apply knowledge and the support to balance freedom with constraints. Dynamic operating systems build on people's trust in their own capabilities, and their trust in others.

The operating system to act (Figure 20) connects all organizational units with a conversation about their performance. As a rich communications process, collaboration makes structures scalable, meaning that with it, organizations can grow without adding more infrastructure. Together, this creates a culture with a shared agenda.

Implementation	**Bureaucracy**	**Self-organization**
Context	Predictability	Uncertainty
Systems	Plans and budgets, performance reports	Resource allocation on demand, flexible targets, agile implementation, business reviews
Leadership	Performance target setting and reviews	Interactive performance conversations
Culture	Trust in processes, individual agenda	Team contributions, shared agenda

FIGURE 20: THE OPERATING SYSTEM TO ACT

Traditional implementation operating systems get things done through bureaucratic processes that work well in highly predictable contexts. Plans, budgets and performance management facilitate target setting and business reviews. It's the traditional managers' means to coordinating work.

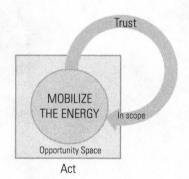

FIGURE 21: IMPLEMENTATION SYSTEMS

Dynamic operating systems for implementation (Figure 21) enable action in self-organized teams when uncertainty is high. Resources are allocated on demand, with flexible plans and decentralized business reviews to support implementation. Leaders interactively challenge teams. Together, this leads to a culture with a shared agenda that facilitates the collaboration.

People-centric principles, agile organizations and dynamic systems resolve the tension between uncertainty and energy. The solution comes from trusting people and their ability to act on their own. Collaboration in self-organized teams offers action despite uncertainty.

LEVER 3: MOBILIZE THE ENERGY

Trust is the means to address uncertainty. Simultaneously, trust grows collaboration.

KEY CHAPTER IDEAS

- Uncertainty requires trust.
- Trust in action is the means for people to address uncertainty.
- At scale, organizations need diversity and trust as the means to collaborate.
- Implementation systems help people mobilize the energy.

ACTION AGENDA

Determine action capabilities and systems to mobilize people to collaborate:

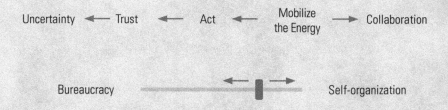

- Understand the degree of uncertainty and need for trust.
- Decide on the principle of mobilizing the energy to fit your context.
- Engage agile techniques for collaboration across boundaries.
- Identify the operating system for action based on trust and collaboration.

FURTHER READING

Sprenger RK (2007). Vertrauen führt – Worauf es in Unternehmen ankommt [Trust Leads – What Matters Most in Organizations], Frankfurt/New York, Campus, 3rd ed.

Galford, R; and Drapeau, AS (2002). *The Trusted Leaders: Bringing out the Best in Your People and Your Company*. New York: The Free Press.

CHAPTER

MAINTAIN THE FOCUS

You know better than anyone how volatile your market is. New opportunities pop up and distract your attention, and the attention of your people, away from your chosen direction. It's hard to maintain focus in a fast-changing context.

People-Centric Management suggests attention as the principle for people to address volatility and the means to learn. Maintaining the focus (Figure 22) is the people-centric solution for organizations looking to scale how people can individually stick to the chosen opportunity when volatility distracts attention.

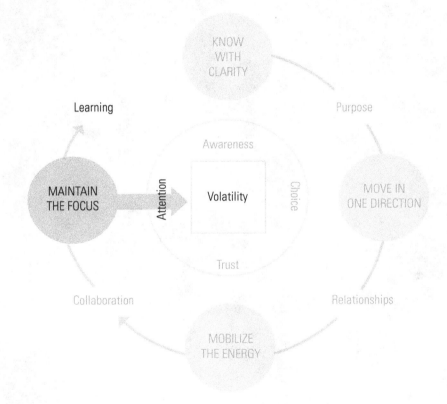

FIGURE 22: MAINTAIN THE FOCUS

This chapter offers the principles, means and systems to resolve the 'focus' tension:

- How do we maintain the focus?
- How do we stick with the chosen opportunity, despite volatility?
- How do we reconcile the tension between volatility and focus?
- How do we enable people to learn?

The solution comes from focusing attention on how people *engage* and *adhere* to maintaining their chosen direction. As such, we'll explore the alternatives for how mangers can help people focus and learn. Then, we'll identify and determine the use of beliefs and boundary systems to facilitate focus of attention and learning at scale, throughout the organization.

Volatility makes it hard to stay on track and follow the chosen path. Agility helps people remain flexible and still stay on track. Maintaining the focus ensures that they have the means to deliver value, even when things change rapidly and frequently.

FOCUS YOUR ATTENTION

How do we maintain the focus? Being able to focus attention is an essential skill for people to learn and perform. Attentive and focused people are better at dealing with a fast-changing environment.

Focus is having self-initiated attention to what matters most. It's a conscious act of concentration that requires energy. The challenge for people is to maintain the focus over a period of time. Managers have the choice between self-initiated focus of attention and goal achievement.

Here is your test:

- Has management created an environment that allows people to focus their skills, abilities and talents to perform their jobs effectively?
- Does management create interferences that prevent people from being able to focus their attention on being effective and productive?

ALTERNATIVES TO MAINTAIN THE FOCUS

How do we reconcile the tension between volatility and focus? Lever 4 (Figure 23) spans traditional, detailed target setting and focus of attention. It's a choice based on how knowledge is distributed in the organization. The choice will require beliefs and boundary systems to help reconcile the tensions. The slider offers the alternatives between detailed targets and attention.

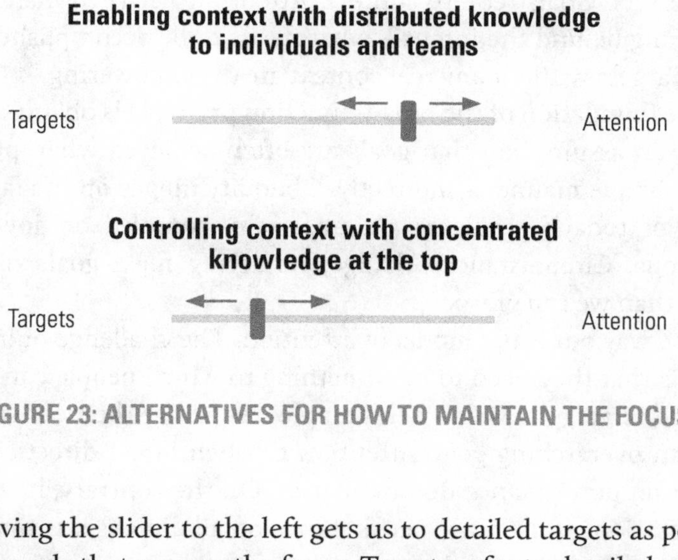

**Enabling context with distributed knowledge
to individuals and teams**

Targets ←|→ Attention

**Controlling context with concentrated
knowledge at the top**

Targets ←|→ Attention

FIGURE 23: ALTERNATIVES FOR HOW TO MAINTAIN THE FOCUS

Moving the slider to the left gets us to detailed targets as performance goals that narrow the focus. Targets refer to detailed performance objectives that limit the scope of the search for opportunities.

This model favours the alignment of goals, performance indicators and rigid strategies. Alignment refers to the pursuit, with others, of one goal, based on a hierarchy of goals, or the need for collaboration. The idea is that everyone in the organization works towards common objectives. Alignment assumes that individuals and organizations have the same agenda. However, it is accepted that people are driven by their own inner purpose and not by detailed performance contracts.

Moreover, alignment requires objectives: measures that combine with incentives to block out everything that is not specifically included. This does not mean alignment is an inferior concept. Being aware of its consequences allows organizations to use the model in the correct context. Targets clearly relate to extrinsically motivated purpose.

Moving the slider to the right asks for focus of attention. Attention requires concentration as the means for people to continuously learn while they search for and capture new opportunities. Attention requires beliefs and boundary systems that guide the focus on the important things.

Leaders often express annual business targets as percentage of growth, or the amount of cost they want to reduce, without any credible articulation of how that contributes to the overall strategy and results. Goals require context. Attention needs to include the reasoning behind the intent – what needs to be accomplished, and why. Targets without any real context are disempowering.

The foundation of the broad-direction principle is obliquity (Kay, 2010), an assumption that goals are often achieved when pursued in an oblique manner – indirectly. Obliquity hinges on the fact that many of today's problems are uncertain, complex or downright nefarious. Circumstances change, rendering fixed goals obsolete faster than we can grasp.

One way out is the model of attention. The challenge of indirect goals is that they need to be something to which people can relate. A broad strategy or vision helps employees bridge their own agenda with an overarching goal. Attention through broad direction does not mean performance doesn't matter. On the contrary, it requires organizations to measure performance on all dimensions that matter. Be aware, however, that organizations often use 'meaning' when they talk about 'extrinsic motivated purpose' (i.e., goals and targets).

LEARN LIKE AN ENTREPRENEUR

Focus of attention is the most effective approach to learning. And learning starts with a fresh look at control.

Managing people is one of the manager's primary functions. Yet, making 'control' work for today's organizations is a challenge. Control must balance competing demands. Individual elements of control are created to resolve the tensions between freedom and constraints, top-down direction and bottom-up creativity, experimentation and efficiency.

Control is defined as any mechanism that managers use to direct attention, motivate, and energize people to act in desired ways and meet organizational objectives. It is the attempt to influence and control others' behaviours through attention. If an individual's attention is not directed towards what needs to be done, the chances of it ever being done are very low. Hence, without attention there is no learning, and there can be no performance. This means that the structuring and management of attention is central to control processes in organizations. Moreover, control needs to resolve the conflict between self-interested behaviours and organizational goals. It needs to reconcile self-interest with the desire to contribute.

Traditional control focuses on the choice of tools from a management perspective. This means leaders select their processes and tools according to the degree to which they understand the transformation process, from input to output. They use it to observe the actions of employees, or to measure the outputs produced. Individuals learn naturally, but bureaucracies are good at blocking that inclination to learn. In the age of 'the modern knowledge worker,' it's time to revert to what we call 'client-focused control' (the client, in this case, being the employee). The task is to structure control in a way that enables creativity and learning, so that it becomes an enabling function.

Entrepreneurs emphasize learning over traditional control. They know intuitively that capturing new things is more important than preserving the old. Successful entrepreneurs continuously learn and innovate by focusing their attention on clients.

As a leader and employee, ask yourself:

- How can I help people feel a sense of accomplishment, feel they're making a difference, and learn?
- How can I act as an entrepreneur to get things done and continuously learn?

People naturally learn. Agile techniques facilitate the learning at scale in organizations.

THE OPERATING SYSTEM TO ENGAGE AND ADHERE

How do we enable people to learn? The operating system to engage and adhere (Figure 24) with beliefs and boundaries enables people to maintain their focus on their search for opportunities.

Beliefs and Boundaries	**Targets**	**Attention**
Context	Stability, knowledge at the top	Volatility, distributed knowledge
Systems	Vision, mission, performance objectives	Beliefs and boundaries (values as verbs)
Leadership	Management by objectives	Interactive contribution dialogue, risk dialogue
Culture	Individual incentives for goal achievement	Shared aspirations and norms

FIGURE 24: THE OPERATING SYSTEM TO ENGAGE AND ADHERE

Beliefs link people to vision, values and meaning, to help them find purpose, and norms tie people to adherence and governance. Beliefs and boundaries set the frame for the things that are within or outside the limits of the opportunity space. The nature of the challenges that the organization has decided to tackle determines much of the design, the use and the impact of these controls. This is why beliefs and boundary systems need to fit your specific situation in order to support People-Centric Management. As with a good car, the brakes and the engine need to be up to handling road conditions and the nature of your intended trip.

Traditional beliefs and boundaries focus people's attention through detailed targets that work well when knowledge is at the top. Vision, mission, and goals set performance targets and offer clarity on what is in and out of scope. Rigorous management by objectives reigns in the organization. Incentive plans ensure that people stick to their targets like rabbits to carrots.

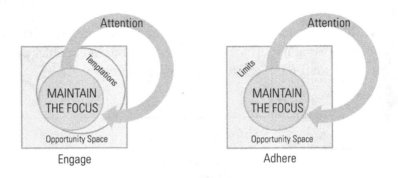

FIGURE 25: BELIEFS AND BOUNDARY SYSTEMS

Dynamic beliefs and boundary systems (Figure 25) enable employee engagement and adherence to aspirations and norms in a context where knowledge and decision-making is distributed throughout the organization. Leaders interact and engage in dialogue on contribution and risks. Shared aspirations and norms create a strong culture at scale.

People-centric principles, agile means and dynamic systems resolve the tension between volatility and focus. The solution comes from helping people focus their attention on what matters most. Learning is the catalyst for people and the organization at scale to stick to chosen opportunities, despite the challenges of higher volatility.

LEVER 4: MAINTAIN THE FOCUS

Focus of attention is the means to address volatility. Simultaneously, focus expedites learning.

KEY CHAPTER IDEAS

- Volatility distracts focus.
- Attention is the means for people to address volatility.
- At scale, an organization needs to provide the means to learn and focus.
- Beliefs and boundary systems help people pay attention.

ACTION AGENDA

Determine engagement and adherence capabilities, and the necessary systems, to maintain the focus and continue to learn:

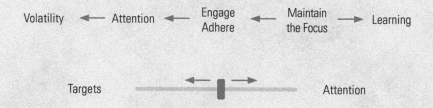

- Understand the degree of volatility and need to focus attention.
- Decide on the principle of maintaining the focus to fit your context.
- Engage agile techniques for faster learning.
- Identify the operating system for engagement and adherence to keep the level of attention.

FURTHER READING

Simons, R (2005). *Levers of Organization Design: How Managers use Accountability Systems for Greater Performance and Commitment.* Harvard Business School Press.

CHAPTER

ALIGNING THE LEVERS

So far, in Chapters 3-6, we have explored the four people-centric levers. To agree on a specific principle is one thing. Aligning multiple principles for the same cause requires one more step. Think of this as a distinct design activity with your management team.

After deciding on the four levers, with clarity on the principles, agile techniques as the means and dynamic operating systems, the next step is to align them with each other to maximize their impact, in line with the predominant operating mode, in response to the specific context.

This chapter offers four operating modes as a powerful response to the challenges and opportunities of the new dynamic business environment. Each mode comes with the capabilities that support the choice, and they are designed for different outcomes.

These four operating modes combine specific capabilities based on the principles, means and systems of your choice. Shifting the levers creates a variety of alignment options (Figure 26).

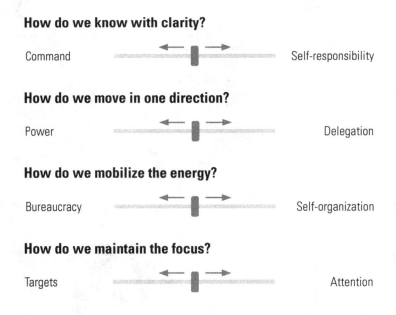

How do we know with clarity?

Command   Self-responsibility

How do we move in one direction?

Power   Delegation

How do we mobilize the energy?

Bureaucracy   Self-organization

How do we maintain the focus?

Targets   Attention

FIGURE 26: ALIGNMENT OPTIONS

By design, there are many possible combinations of these levers, achieved by simply moving the sliders. However, from our research we know that four combinations of capabilities are needed to cover most business cases.

For this discussion, we need a deeper understanding of what we call operating modes. They present four distinct ways to manage people and organizations. First, we select systems and leadership as the controls that facilitate management. Second, we separate traditional from people-centric and dynamic managerial responses. The result of these combinations is four operating modes, as mapped in Figure 27.

FIGURE 27: FOUR OPERATING MODES

Leadership and systems within the framework can have four operating modes: control, engagement, change and enabling. With systems, organizations respond to the changing business context with VUCA. Leadership is the answer to the needs of knowledge among people in the changing work environment.

Four questions (Figure 28) determine your dominant mode:

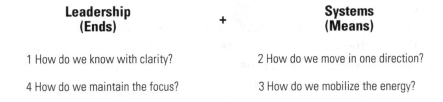

**Leadership
(Ends)**
+
**Systems
(Means)**

1 How do we know with clarity?   2 How do we move in one direction?

4 How do we maintain the focus?   3 How do we mobilize the energy?

FIGURE 28: TWO ALIGNMENT TASKS

Leadership is managerial control through interaction. Its goal is to serve people, the ultimate ends of management. Systems represent managerial control through the institution. They are the means of management. As such, systems as means are always in support of people – the ends. Figure 29 aligns the levers for the enabling mode.

In organizations where knowledge is distributed, agile leadership ensures that people know with clarity (Lever 1) and maintain their focus (Lever 4) in order to unlock the talent of people. Engagement or enabling modes apply. In a dynamic environment, organizations apply dynamic systems that help them quickly move in one direction (Lever 2) and mobilize the energy (Lever 3) in order to capture opportunities or not risk disruption. Change or enabling modes apply. People-centric leadership and dynamic systems align to the enabling mode.

Traditional means of control are appropriate in some circumstances, but not in others. In an increasingly dynamic environment, firms can build competitive advantage by engaging agile systems and empowering employees at the client interface rather than trying to control and command them. Rapid recognition of contextual change, and change in knowledge distribution, become synonymous with the practices that facilitate organizational learning. This is why we complement the control approach with change, engagement and enabling management approaches.

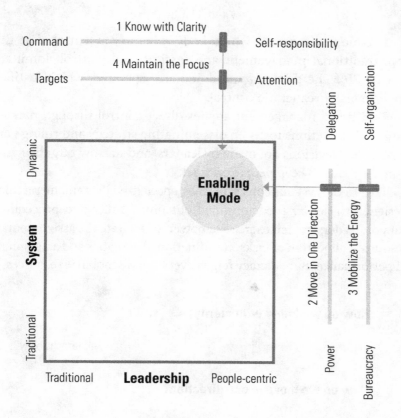

FIGURE 29: ALIGNING THE LEVERS

The operating framework now serves as the alignment tool for levers with systems that articulate the four operating modes.

CONTROL

In a stable environment where knowledge is concentrated at the top, traditional management and institutional control dominate (Figure 30). The thinking and doing are separated, which justifies traditional, bureaucratic control.

Traditional management applies direct control through narrow targets. Interactions focus on disseminating strategy and ruling performance. Decisions are made by leaders, and narrow targets maintain the focus to keep people on track.

Traditional systems consist of rules, specialized jobs and hierarchies designed to deliver predetermined outcomes. Rules and procedures support leaders in their exercise of power to facilitate the assignment of resources, allocation of tasks, coordination of activities and assessment of performance. Bureaucracy reigns over how we mobilize resources.

How do we know with clarity?

Command — Self-responsibility

How do we move in one direction?

Power — Delegation

How do we mobilize the energy?

Bureaucracy — Self-organization

How do we maintain the focus?

Targets — Attention

Means: Ends:
Systems   Leadership

FIGURE 30: CONTROL MODE

Control offers a stable organizational platform. For example, imagine flying an airplane. No passenger would want the pilot to become creative and innovative in his job. The expectation is that he follows clear standards and rules. Yet, in an emergency, any passenger would expect the pilot to apply his knowledge to address the problem.

A stable control platform is, in many contexts, a prerequisite for higher organizational agility. Consequently, companies can blend the control mode with other approaches, as the context requires.

When leaders want to do something that may be impossible, control puts a constraint on command. When leaders know something that needs to get done and can be done, then harder work is necessary, and command needs control. Both control and command are necessary, and often beyond the traditional control mode.

ENGAGEMENT

In a knowledge-driven environment with little change, the engagement mode (Figure 31) dominates. People (the ends) are tightly controlled by traditional means.

How do we know with clarity?

Command ———————————————— Self-responsibility

How do we move in one direction?

Power ———————————————— Delegation

How do we mobilize the energy?

Bureaucracy ———————————————— Self-organization

How do we maintain the focus?

Targets ———————————————— Attention

Means: Systems   Ends: Leadership

FIGURE 31: ENGAGEMENT MODE

People-Centric Management supports self-responsible people guided by focus of attention. Management aligns individual interests through visions, beliefs, boundaries and values. As Harvard Business School's Robert Simons (1995) put it, "In the absence of management action, self-interested behaviour at the expense of organizational goals is inevitable." Self-responsibility and attention are balanced with hierarchical power and institutional bureaucracy.

Traditional systems control information, provide direction, coordinate work and allocate resources. Power, hierarchy and bureaucracy tightly control what people do. Traditional means meet people-centric ends.

It's a mix that works in a stable context, but cannot with greater VUCA. Well-intended HR initiatives create a better work environment but fail to support an organization that competes in a dynamic market context.

Engagement means management interaction. It's a mode where leaders need to spend less time with their laptops and more time with the people at the client front, engaged in a creative process. It's about helping people make sense of what they're asked to do, how things can be done, and how that fits with the overall strategy. Leaders cannot assume that people know. Leaders need to help them make sense of things.

Data is not the same as onsite experience. A leader who really wants to know what's going on at the client front needs to be there, not cloistered away in his home office, hunched over his 'control' desktop. You may have all the data but still lack the feel for things.

CHANGE

In a dynamic market environment with centralized decision-making, direct intervention with the change mode (Figure 32) dominates. Dynamic systems (the means) meet traditional ways to lead people (the ends).

Change modes operate through a market control setting where managers alter the resource base, align interests through incentives and restructure accountabilities in response to market changes.

These organizations apply rigorous targets, tying people and teams to outcomes that align with the firm's overall performance objectives. Such organizations favour disciplined, one-step change programmes to adapt their organization to changes in the environment. It's the traditional way to react to the new context: delegating change but keeping control of it.

How do we know with clarity?

Command — Self-responsibility

How do we move in one direction?

Power — Delegation

How do we mobilize the energy?

Bureaucracy — Self-organization

How do we maintain the focus?

Targets — Attention

Ends: Leadership   Means: Systems

FIGURE 32: CHANGE MODE

ENABLING

In a dynamic context with knowledge distributed throughout the organization, the enabling mode (Figure 33) dominates. People-centric leadership (the ends) and dynamic systems (the means) match.

How do we know with clarity?

Command — Self-responsibility

How do we move in one direction?

Power — Delegation

How do we mobilize the energy?

Bureaucracy — Self-organization

How do we maintain the focus?

Targets — Attention

Means: Systems   Ends: Leadership

FIGURE 33: ENABLING MODE

In dynamic and enabling contexts, traditional rules-based management approaches are not effective. Under these conditions, enabling modes support fast decision-making and proactive, flexible action, which lead to robust outcomes.

Self-managed workgroups and wider spans of control decrease the importance of direct managerial influence and increase the interpersonal influence and lateral coordination to direct and motivate work. This requires peer control as the process, where peers direct attention, motivate and encourage performance.

Enabling mode organizations require people-centric managerial competencies and a talent base that favours creativity and continuous innovation. Learning, and access to knowledge through networks, is as essential as their approach to continuously reassessing their resource base. Change is ongoing, but not as a disruptive process. It is the dynamic systems capability that makes these organizations agile and nimble.

The following chapter, The Enabling Mode, expands the concept with people-centric principles, agile capabilities and dynamic systems to make people-centric work. The enabling mode is the ultimate response to the business context in the 21st century.

Control, engagement, change and enabling modes align with the challenges of the external environment and the distribution of knowledge. Adjusting the levers and applying the corresponding capabilities, principles and tools creates adequate responses to these challenges.

Over our 20 years of work with clients, and through corresponding research, we've discovered combinations of levers that do not work. Misaligned levers create all sorts of interferences that require our attention.

FAULTY LEADERSHIP

Think of well-intended, self-responsible leadership style meets traditional management. It's the situation where leaders demand that people take charge, decide and get things done, while at the same time narrowing their focus by applying traditional, detailed management by objectives. Narrow targets limit people's ability to take self-responsible action. I call this faulty leadership (Figure 34).

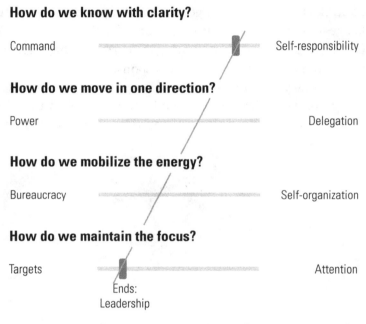

How do we know with clarity?

Command   Self-responsibility

How do we move in one direction?

Power   Delegation

How do we mobilize the energy?

Bureaucracy   Self-organization

How do we maintain the focus?

Targets   Attention

Ends:
Leadership

FIGURE 34: FAULTY LEADERSHIP

Recently, I was able to work with the CEO of a large cosmetics company. When I walked into his office building, I immediately noticed a respectful, modern leadership style where people were asked to take charge. It was in the air, and deeply embedded in their culture. The task was to talk about agility and find out what could be done about it.

With the results from our Diagnostic[8] with the cosmetics company, we noticed the misalignment of two people-centric levers: know with clarity and maintain the focus. The Diagnostic revealed that the organization maintained a management by objectives system that forced leaders to hammer out detailed objective agreements and conduct rigorous performance reviews with their people. With the insights from the Diagnostic, and no need to further convince, the CEO decided to work on the system and fundamentally revamp their current management by objectives process to align with his way of working with self-responsible people.

MISSING LEADERSHIP

Control needs to meet attention, or we let it go. This is leadership that wants to be in control but does not deliver sufficient direction and guidance. People are left to follow orders without knowing why and how. If you feel that this is an infrequent combination, you'd be wrong. Missing leadership (Figure 35) does not so much come from leaders' inability to do better – it is the consequence of systemically under-managed organizations, for example, in their early growth phase.

Consider the dominant inventor of a new medical device and founder of his firm. While he was successful with the start-up, after three years growth had slowed and managerial challenges limited the firm's capabilities. We were asked to come and have a look at the situation. The Diagnostic highlighted the usual misalignment we see in most growth firms. The dominant leader was not able to directly influence all employees with his message. And, he'd neglected to introduce institutional systems that would support his style. As his direct influence and visibility vanished, there was nothing to back it up. Attention was entirely left to individuals. As a consequence, they all went off in their own direction. The fix was simple: he introduced simple tools, with sufficient guidance, for people to follow him even when he was remotely located. That's leadership.

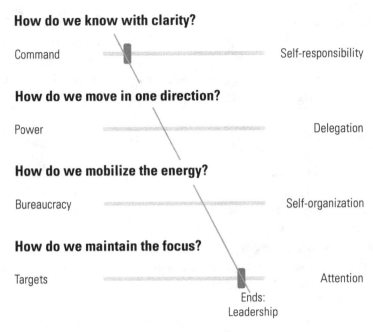

How do we know with clarity?

Command — Self-responsibility

How do we move in one direction?

Power — Delegation

How do we mobilize the energy?

Bureaucracy — Self-organization

How do we maintain the focus?

Targets — Attention

Ends:
Leadership

FIGURE 35: MISSING LEADERSHIP

OUT OF CONTROL

When power and self-organization meet, then organizations are out of control (Figure 36). Leaders, teams and individuals demand to be in control. As we know, too many cooks spoil the broth. When self-organized teams meet power and hierarchy, interferences are pre-programmed. Direction and resource allocation don't align.

Things spiral out of control when leaders with big strategy announcements converge with the allocation of resources to 'he who cries the most.' I remember being called into an executive meeting where the leader announced his new strategy for the years ahead. It was the sort of meeting where the entire team was present, but merely there to approve the grand idea. Before the session was over, resources were allocated to two dominant voices. Other participants were puzzled. I then asked what about those units that were not present. "It's self-organization," I was told. "That's our culture."

To align central strategy with decentralized implementation, the organization had to turn the self-serving of resources into a structured process, where resources were allocated on demand to the units that needed them to implement their strategy. That system, in return, changed the culture of the firm.

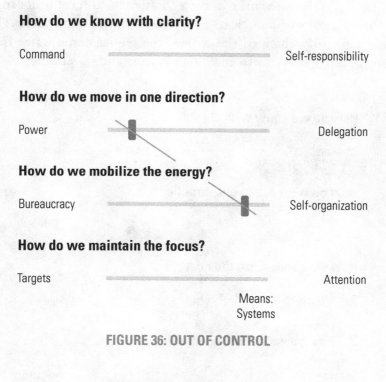

How do we know with clarity?

Command ———————————————— Self-responsibility

How do we move in one direction?

Power ————————————————— Delegation

How do we mobilize the energy?

Bureaucracy ———————————————— Self-organization

How do we maintain the focus?

Targets ———————————————— Attention

Means:
Systems

FIGURE 36: OUT OF CONTROL

ERRONEOUS SYSTEMS

When delegated decision-making meets central bureaucracy, people have two options: ignore central guidance or cheat the system. Both behaviours are unacceptable from a central perspective, and they eventually lead to an infected culture. But, they are the normal behaviours of decentralized units when bureaucracy limits delegated authority. The cause is erroneous systems (Figure 37). If you find yourself there, it's time to reinvent the system.

In this example, a large financial services institution switched its business model from a central approach to one that entailed many disparate business units around the world. The CEO was clear from the beginning that decentralized decision-making would not work in a traditional environment, where bureaucracy prevailed.

So, he fundamentally changed the way the organization measured performance, developed strategy, managed performance, set targets and dealt with risks that bureaucracy posed for self-organized units. He put frameworks in place that enabled local units to do it themselves, within a clear set of rules, routines and tools. That simultaneously changed the role of the global home office from controlling operations to enabling business and governance.

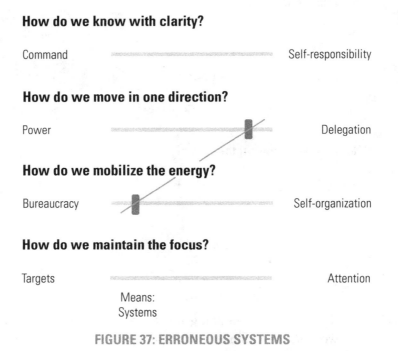

How do we know with clarity?

Command .... Self-responsibility

How do we move in one direction?

Power .... Delegation

How do we mobilize the energy?

Bureaucracy .... Self-organization

How do we maintain the focus?

Targets .... Attention

Means:
Systems

FIGURE 37: ERRONEOUS SYSTEMS

The Leadership Toolbox – a grid that helps people understand, think, deliver, engage and adhere – provided the organization with a set of techniques and actions that made it agile and fast. It offered as simple way to scale business. (We'll examine the Leadership Toolbox in detail in the pages ahead.)

The operating modes framework offers four ways to align the levers and design leadership and systems accordingly. The framework also helps leaders prevent a setup of levers that does not work.

Knowing that can avert falling into known design traps. Figure 38 summarizes four proven operating modes.

Operating Modes	Control	Change	Engagement	Enabling
1 Know with Clarity	Command	Command	Self-responsibility	Self-responsibility
2 Move in One Direction	Bureaucracy	Self-organization	Bureaucracy	Self-organization
3 Mobilize the Energy	Power	Delegation	Power	Delegation
4 Maintain the Focus	Targets	Targets	Attention	Attention
Leadership	Traditional		People-centric	
Systems	Traditional	Dynamic	Traditional	Dynamic

FIGURE 38: DOMINANT OPERATING MODES

So far, we have assumed that a lever is either traditional or people-centric. When we assess operating modes with the Diagnostic, or offer advice on ideal operating modes, they are more often than not hybrids. Levers tend towards traditional or people-centric and combining levers more or less results in traditional or people-centric. In our experience, operating modes must work in practice and fit the specific context of the business. They are always hybrids, with more or less of one or the other mode.

In addition, we have assumed that organizations come with one operations mode. The reality is that most organizations operate with more than one mode. They coexist within the same organization. Multiple modes in one organization work well when it's done deliberately, and with separate designs of principles, means and systems.

Imagine the operation of a hospital. It always operates in a dual mode. Normal operations follow the engagement mode. Emergency operations follow the control mode for normal procedures, but often flip to the enabling mode when experience and knowledge are needed quickly to deal with non-routine cases. In hospitals, people are trained to operate in multiple modes, with systems that support each mode.

In this chapter, we've explored how to align and combine levers to fit the specific context and the requirements of the new work environment with distributed knowledge. The right combination of these levers is what creates value in organizations.

ALIGNING THE LEVERS

Using the context framework to decide on the dominant operating mode, and align levers to support an integrated operating mode, as a powerful response to challenges and opportunities.

KEY CHAPTER IDEAS

Operating modes are distinctive ways to organize and manage organizations in line with the specific context and distribution of knowledge.
- Align the levers to fit one of the four operating modes
- Prevent misalignment of levers, as this creates interferences
- Operating modes come with specific principles, means and systems

ACTION AGENDA

To manage in the people-centric way, clarify your choice of operating mode:
- Understand your current mode of operations
- Decide on your desired mode of operations
- Design your operating system to match your choice

FURTHER READING

Michel, L; Anzengruber, J; Wölfle, M; and Hixson, N (2018). Under What Conditions do Rules-Based and Capability-Based Management Modes Dominate? *Special Issue Risks in Financial and Real Estate Markets Journal*, 6(32).

Dood, D; and Favaro, K (2006). Managing the Right Tensions. *Harvard Business Review*, December.

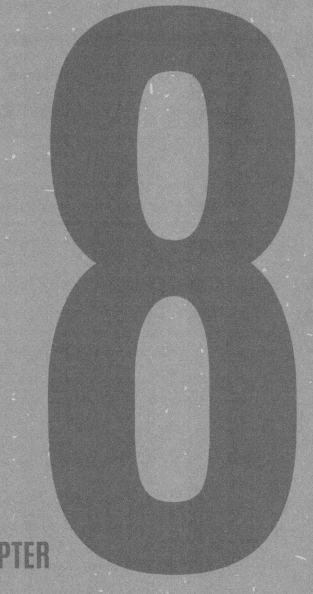

CHAPTER

THE
ENABLING
MODE

Following our overview of the four operating modes in the previous chapter, it's now time to dig deep into the agile capabilities that make up the enabling mode through people-centric leadership and dynamic systems.

We know from experience what the control mode feels like, and how to operate it. This is why we'll now focus less on *the known* than on the more important enabling mode. Think of enabling as a capability that creates a work environment where people unlock their full talent.

Chapter 8 offers the Performance Triangle model, which explores the elements of an agile organization. With the Leadership Scorecard, we extend the elements to add a managerial perspective. In combination, this will offer the agile capabilities that are needed to operate in the enabling mode.

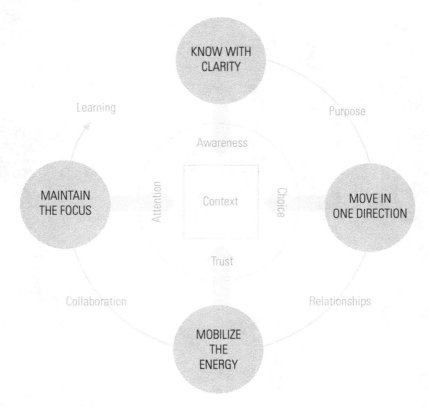

FIGURE 39: FOUR LEVERS WITH AGILE CAPABILITIES

Four levers (Figure 39) frame the enabling mode with agile capabilities. The enabling mode establishes awareness, choice, trust and attention as the people-centric principles to address the dynamic context at the centre. It encompasses the following:

- **Know with clarity** for self-responsible action
- **Move in one direction** with distributed accountability
- **Mobilize the energy** to enable self-organization
- **Maintain the focus** through attention

So far, we have discussed two ways to establish the enabling mode: individual leadership and institutional systems.

We now need to add culture, which serves as the glue for the enabling mode. We do this with the help of the Performance Triangle model. It is extensively documented in *The Performance Triangle: Diagnostic Mentoring to Manage Organizations and People for Superior Performance in Turbulent Times* (Michel, 2013). The triangle allows us to look at every angle of the levers and translate the alternatives into systems, leadership and culture requirement.

With the Performance Triangle, we review organizational agility as a means to establish the engagement mode. And with the Leadership Scorecard, we add the management perspective. Organization and management combine as the operating system with agile features, creating a culture with a shared mindset, interactive leadership skill set and diagnostic management systems as the toolset. In combination, the Performance Triangle and the Leadership Scorecard frame agile capabilities.

THE ENABLING
OPERATING ENVIRONMENT

The Performance Triangle models the enabling operating environment (Figure 40) with culture, leadership and systems at its corners and success on top. Effective agile actions require a culture that creates shared context. Leadership is interactive, to facilitate the conversations around purpose, direction and performance. Systems work diagnostically, with direct attention to those aspects that matter most, allowing for self-directed action on deviations from the chosen path. Shared context, people interactions and diagnostic controls make up the capabilities of an agile organization. Together, they help people detect weak signals early, allow for the interpretation of that information, and facilitate timely action.

Here are the elements of an enabling organization:
- **The operating environment:** culture, leadership, systems
- **The individual environment:** people with the inner game
- **The work environment:** purpose, collaboration, relationships

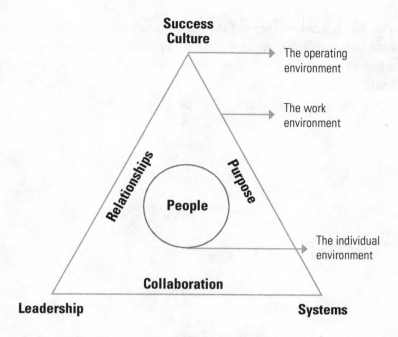

FIGURE 40: THE ENABLING ORGANIZATION

The individual environment. People are at the centre of the triangle. Awareness, choice, trust and attention are the means for people to perform at their peak. They are the capabilities that enable speed. When people apply these four capabilities, leaders can delegate work at the client front. As a result, decisions are made where the work is being done, which accelerates decisions and action.

The operating environment. The corners with leadership, systems and culture enable agility. Interactive leadership is about the personal interaction between leaders and employees. Diagnostic systems offer the rules, routines and tools to get work done. Culture represents the invisible guide and glue. When leaders connect and interact with employees, systems offer guidance and feedback, and culture establishes strong bonds, then agile is at its peak.

The work environment. Purpose, relationships and collaboration establish resilience. When people find purpose in what they're doing, when they collaborate across boundaries, and when they connect to build relationships that enhance their knowledge, then organizations can resist any external shocks. They are resilient.

PEOPLE

For higher agility, people need to be at the centre of your attention. To come to this conclusion, we need to make the following assumption: since European Humanism in the 18th century, people have been seen as responsible, critical, self-developing individuals. They want to contribute, learn and grow. However, there's no such thing as the image of mankind. We are all different, unique and mostly irrational. But this generalization helps us better deal with the fissure between what people need to perform well and the current reality of control in most organizations.

Indisputably, people are central to creating an agile organization. And in agile organizations, the true value of people is in their relationships, interactions and collaboration.

To get things done, people require competencies in five areas: understand, think, act, adhere and engage (Figure 41). This is in line with Drucker (1967): "In the knowledge age, employees become executives." That is to say, they make decisions.

Understand. Information and immediate feedback raise awareness of what is important. This helps people understand what matters and focuses attention. Superior understanding requires that sensors are not on mute and amplifiers work properly.

Think. Knowledge people have a set of mental maps. These help them make sense of situations and make decisions. The benefits for an organization come not only from individual thinking, but also from collective thinking. The thinking requires an opportunity to create meaning and asks for a deliberate choice to move in one direction.

Act. Translating ideas into action. The task is to mobilize the energy to get things done. People put their energy into things that they care about. And energy requires action to be meaningful. Contribution requires the opportunity to apply knowledge and support, and to balance freedom and constraints. Superior contributions build on the trust of people and in people.

Engage. Attention is a limited resource, and energy is required to maintain it at a high level. Attention must be focused to prevent distraction from competing demands. A high level of engagement requires beliefs, motives and purpose.

Adhere. Energy adds 'pull' and a positive tension to the boundaries of an organization. This tension requires a balance between entrepreneurship and efficiency. A high level of adherence maintains a good balance.

	Understand	Think	Act	Engage	Adhere
Employees	Require feedback on where the work is being done	Make decisions	Are motivated by a sense of purpose	Have clear priorities	Are empowered and clear about norms
Challenges	Unlimited information	Unlimited opportunities; encouraged to take risks	Increased pressures	Limited attention; limited resources	Growing temptations
Traditions	Information is limited to the top	Leaders making decision	Leaders motivate for performance	Employees execute	… and control what gets done
Interferences	Lack of information	Lack of opportunities; fear of risk	Lack of purpose	Conflicting goals; lack of resources	Lack of boundaries

FIGURE 41: PEOPLE POTENTIAL AND INTERFERENCES

In *Levers of Control* (1995), Professor Robert Simons of Harvard Business School states: "To unleash this potential [knowledge people] managers must overcome organizational blocks. Management control systems play an important role in this process." Over the years, organizational 'viruses' have invaded many firms, introducing interferences in the form of faulty leadership, erroneous systems or an infected culture, preventing people from performing at their peak. Or, as framed by Gallwey (2000): "The greater the external challenges accepted by a company, team or individual, the more important it is that there is minimum interference occurring from within."

Performance and creativity require degrees of freedom, self-responsibility and the ability to focus. These are things that are not naturally given in organizations, even though every responsible leader would insist that 'everything is under control.' Control is the key word for the lack of understanding of what performance is all about. Humanism, propounded by the Enlightenment philosopher Immanuel Kant, introduced the notion of "Humans as the end, not the means." This means that people should not be used to reach higher goals. Creativity, freely interpreted, requires fairness (equality), individualism and an elevated sense of purpose of work. Kant calls these the attributes of a modern society.

Translated into the reality of today's organizations, this means that responsible employees require choice, trust and purpose to innovate and perform. The enabling mode assumes that people are self-motivated and want to get things done. This calls for providing them with observation points to focus their attention. Higher awareness means they sense early signs and have a significant degree of freedom to react to them. Choice is the foundation for responsibility. Once people have made their choices, they will need to be trusted to maintain the right focus. The inner game techniques translate knowledge into action and require an enabling working environment.

LEADERSHIP

Leadership is a key component of the triangle. In today's organizations, be they a small group in a traditional structure, a community or an ecosystem, leadership is exercised wherever it influences other people's thinking, behaviours, decisions and actions. Leadership is not necessarily tied to traditional positions with power in hierarchies. Effective leaders in agile organizations interact with people on a personal level, relate to others to facilitate meaningful collaboration and establish a supportive work environment based on a culture of trust. In the broadest sense, leadership is communication and interaction with others at all levels, vertically and horizontally, throughout an organization. We suggest that leaders in any organization develop effective communication and interaction skills that are natural and unique to them.

The traditional notion is that the culture of an organization is shaped from the top of the management hierarchy and cascades downwards. We generally accept this belief. However, we have seen in many organizations a huge disconnect between what top executives *think* is going on and what the rank and file employees actually believe.

Leaders and managers at all levels must recognize that their actions and behaviours are being observed and interpreted by employees through the lenses of their own beliefs and values. Many leaders, perhaps inadvertently, fail to connect with employees, and they communicate conflicting values and beliefs throughout the organization. Employees will rarely approach the CEO and say: 'You said (this), but we actually did (that). Which is it, and what's going on?' The result is that employees are left to develop their own interpretation, which is in many cases inconsistent with organizational goals.

Leading requires fluency in things that are unnatural to us. Teaming and interactions mean that leaders take interpersonal risks.

True teaming requires a sense of psychological safety, and stepping back to see others' perspectives. It's about losing traditional control to gain real control.

Leadership is a complex and indefinable quality, but we've identified five unconscious (and rarely discussed) attributes that contribute to strengthening the culture and performance of the organization.

Five conversations can be had, as interactions to exercise leadership control (Figure 42):

1. **Sense-making discussion,** to understand and know with clarity
2. **Strategy level-set,** to think and move in one direction
3. **Performance conversation,** to act and mobilize the energy
4. **Contribution dialogue,** to engage and maintain the focus
5. **Risk discussion,** to adhere to and maintain the focus

FIGURE 42: INTERACTIVE LEADERSHIP

So, what's covered in these conversations?

- **Sense-making.** Do leaders and employees have the capability to sense changes in internal and external environments and interpret their meaning?
- **Strategy.** Do leaders and employees have an understanding of why the organization has established strategic goals, and are goals founded on lessons from the past?
- **Performance.** Do leaders and employees have a clear understanding of whether the organization is on track, what needs to be done to remain on track, and how to achieve superior performance?
- **Contribution.** Do leaders and employees have a clear understanding of what they can do to move the organization forward? Do leaders clearly understand their role?
- **Risk.** Do leaders and employees have a clear understanding of the potential risks, and the ultimate level of risk, the organization can tolerate?

People-Centric Management is *high-touch* interaction with people. Remember, leadership is a contact sport. Yet, when you show up, it's often seen as an interference or interruption. Employees have to worry about clients, not leaders. It's therefore important to show up as encouragement. Encouragements show that we are here for clients. Leadership presence is important.

SYSTEMS

Systems are located at the lower-right corner of the triangle. They represent the institutional toolbox, with rules, routines and resources that set the stage for rigorous and disciplined leadership. It's about systems support implementation with the right balance between freedom and constraint. Supporting collaboration between people and systems provides the fuel to power the formation of beliefs and decisions. This is essential for identifying purpose. In addition, systems set boundaries to achieve the desired balance between entrepreneurship and efficiency.

Systems are both influenced by and influence the culture and leadership practices that shape the decision-making process. When we talk about systems, we aren't just talking about IT systems, but the rules and routines that shape the input and output from computerized tools. Everyone reading this chapter is familiar with the phrases 'garbage in, garbage out' and 'what gets measured, gets done.' However, we contend that such thinking is just scratching the surface of the complex dimension we call 'systems.' What managers and employees do with the output from IT systems, and how that output shapes decisions and behaviours, is rarely considered.

Similarly, we've witnessed many examples of systems developed in prior decades being used to drive decisions today, despite the fact that both the world and the business dynamic are dramatically different. We have seen many instances where managers created systems to generate relevant data needed to solve some problem, or give the organization an edge, 20 years ago. The problem was solved, partially with the aid of the data, and the company gained an edge over competitors.

Today, though, managers are making decisions using information that is no longer relevant, because the problem was solved decades ago and the competitive dynamics have changed significantly.

What was relevant and meaningful 20 years ago may not be today, leading to regrettable decisions. It therefore becomes imperative for leaders to constantly evaluate whether the rules, routines and tools being used to drive decisions are relevant, and whether they shape desired behaviours.

We have identified five questions, the answers to which provide insight into unconscious and rarely examined beliefs, values and shared assumptions that either inhibit or enable the effectiveness of systems.

The system of work and the system of management are interconnected. Changing the system of work will not yield performance if the operating system that governs it remains flawed.

These five diagnostic systems (Figure 43) support people to get work done with the benefit of:

1. **Information** – to understand and know with clarity
2. **Strategy** – to think and move in one direction
3. **Implementation** – to act and mobilize the energy
4. **Beliefs** – to engage and maintain the focus
5. **Boundaries** – to adhere to and maintain the focus

FIGURE 43: DIAGNOSTIC SYSTEMS

Consider the following diagnostic questions to review your systems:

- **Information.** Do leaders and employees at all levels have access to timely and relevant information, to keep them abreast of what's going on inside and outside the organization and help them make informed decisions?
- **Strategy.** Do leaders and employees clearly understand the rules of the game and what's needed to move in one direction?
- **Implementation.** Do leaders and employees throughout the organization clearly understand what is needed to mobilize the energy and implement the strategy?
- **Beliefs.** Do leaders and employees throughout the organization have a shared ambition to adhere to the focus, as determined by the strategy?
- **Boundaries.** Do leaders and employees throughout the organization have a firm understanding of boundaries or limits to their decisions or authority?

CULTURE

The culture of an organization creates shared context, enables or inhibits knowledge exchange, and defines the invisible boundaries of collaboration. A vibrant culture establishes shared context as the common ground, with a shared agenda, language, thought models, relationships and purpose. Shared context is all about a shared mindset, the behaviour of individuals based on common thinking and shared norms. The organizational culture becomes the invisible force that, like gravity, shapes all interactions within the universe in which the organization exists.

We agree with the assertion that culture has two major components – visible and invisible – underlying beliefs, values and shared assumptions that shape the collective thoughts. They can be observed through decisions, behaviours and actions of the people in the organization. Culture has a stabilizing effect on the organization and helps people make things meaningful and predictable.

Each organization has a unique culture that evolves over years and is reinforced as people absorb, repeat and pass along what works. There may be an infinite number of dimensions that make up the culture of an organization, but we've identified five attributes that seem to be nearly universal and thrive, unseen, in the minds and actions of employees at all levels of the organization. These five attributes help form a shared context within the organization.

These five culture elements, which establish a shared mindset, include (Figure 44):

1. **Shared understanding** to know with clarity
2. **Shared intent** to move in one direction
3. **Shared agenda** to mobilize the energy
4. **Shared aspirations** to maintain the focus
5. **Shared norms** to maintain the focus

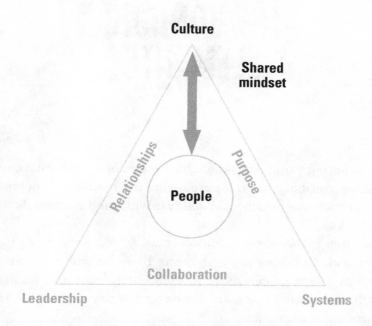

FIGURE 44: SHARED MINDSET CULTURE

- **Understanding.** Do leaders and employees share an understanding of where the organization is and where it is going (or attempting to go)?
- **Intent.** Do leaders and employees share a common intent to how to move the organization forward to meet goals and objectives?
- **Agenda.** Do leaders and employees share a common agenda on what needs to be done to move the organization forward?
- **Aspirations.** Do leaders and employees share a common sense of energy and resources needed to implement strategy?
- **Norms.** Do leaders and employees share a common set of norms of behaviour needed to maintain the chosen focus?

It is important to note that changing culture is more than changing individual mindsets. It's about the collective behaviours as a sort of habit system. Such systems can only be changed by action, experience and feedback, attained through experience, rather than the cognitive abstractions of new values. This is why culture is an outcome, with systems and leadership as its triggers.

THE BONDING
ELEMENTS

In a connected world beyond the boundaries of organizations, relationships, collaboration and purpose are the bonding elements for superior resilience, which is the ability to withstand external changes and shocks.

Isolation is the worst condition at work, and work needs to be meaningful. Collaboration and connectivity become the primary means by which people relate to each other, learn and stimulate growth. The smaller teams are, the easier it is to establish that kind of a working environment.

THE LEADERSHIP
SCORECARD

The Leadership Scorecard (Figure 45) summarizes 20 elements as observation points into a table intended to help leaders work *in* the system. The horizontal view of the scorecard represents the organization view (success, culture, leadership, systems) while the vertical view (information, strategy, implementation, beliefs and boundaries) establishes the management dimension.

The scorecard offers a template with 20 questions to discuss the management view of the Performance Triangle. These elements become context-related and specific through the answers to these questions.

Effective information systems help raise awareness of, and help employees make sense of, what is important. This increases the agility of the organization, as employees can react on changes in the environment.

Clarity of strategy supports leaders in providing direction and establishing a shared intent. This enhances the overall alignment of the organization. Rigorous implementation and performance conversations establish the shared agenda, to address the capabilities of the organization. Strong beliefs enable the conversation about the contribution of every employee. This creates the shared aspirations and purpose for higher motivation. And clear boundaries with a conversation about risks help the organization set its norms. As a result, the organization ensures that it is smart about how it uses its playing field.

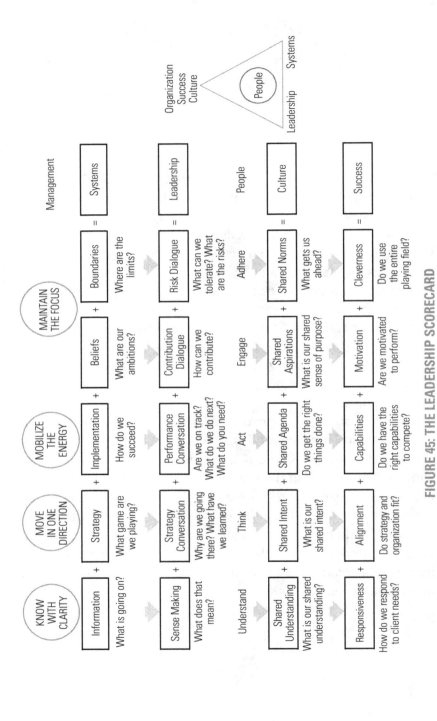

FIGURE 45: THE LEADERSHIP SCORECARD

Imagine driving a car. It takes five things to do that:

First, you need a dashboard that indicates how fast you are going. In organizations, this helps you make sense of information, to create the shared understanding of how well you are doing. → Supporting the ability to understand

Second, the navigation system directs you to the destination. In organizations, the conversation about the strategy creates a shared intent with the team on what direction to take. → Supporting the ability to think

Third, the engine and wheels translate the energy into motion. In organizations, this means implementation – putting the strategy into a shared agenda that plots out what's being done to get there. → Supporting the ability to act

Fourth, with the gas pedal, the driver controls speed. In organizations, acceleration happens through a conversation on beliefs: the vision, mission and individual goals that create pull. → Supporting the ability to engage

Fifth, every car needs brakes. They ensure that speed remains under control and enables the proper reaction to sudden, unexpected events. In organizations, this function resides with boundaries – the governance, structures and risk limits that clarify what is in and out of bounds. → Supporting the ability to adhere

SUCCESS

Success stands at the top of the Performance Triangle, representing the ultimate goal of management. Successful firms meet or exceed expectations by making performance visible in the form of socially accepted outcomes.

In the Performance Triangle model, five attributes determine success: agility as the ability to sense opportunities and react on them; alignment of the organization with strategy as a prerequisite to creating value; organizational core competencies as the foundation for sustainable competitive advantage; motivation of the team to get things done; and the wisdom of how the organization defines and uses its boundaries. These attributes define the primary intangible value-creating elements of an organization, which drive success.

- **Responsiveness.** Is the organization flexible and able to react to changes in the environment?
- **Alignment.** Is the direction of the organization clear? Does the structure fit the strategy? Is it shared broadly, and are employees aligned to support the strategies?
- **Capabilities.** Does the organization have the competencies and skills needed to deliver on promises?
- **Motivation.** Are employees throughout the organization inspired to perform above and beyond expectations?
- **Cleverness.** Are employees empowered to be creative, and to use their creativity to meet expectations or demands from customers within boundaries that do not stifle creativity?

If the answer to these questions is yes, these are signs that People-Centric Management with agile capabilities is creating value.

SPEED, AGILITY AND RESILIENCE

The Performance Triangle represents an organization's operating environment with speed, agility and resilience as its ultimate outcomes. They represent key dynamic capabilities – the mode that enables people and organizations to compete in a dynamic environment.

- **Speed.** The 'individual environment' defines the policy governing how we engage people. The 'inner game' is the tool that helps people translate knowledge into action. It transfers control to the learner. Learning is the solution for time-critical action in dynamic times. Trust and choice further relate the 'people frame' to speed and creative capabilities.
- **Agility.** The 'operating environment' defines the policy for how we coordinate work. Agility is all about sensing opportunities early, taking action, and facilitating continuous change through an integrated organization. It promotes self-organized work in teams, with delegated decision-making for higher flexibility, effective adaptation to external change, improved problem-solving, and superior innovation. Agility requires the combination of dynamic managerial capabilities and managerial controls.
- **Resilience.** The 'work environment' defines the policy for how we establish goals as a bonding element in relationships. It has a stabilizing effect through social controls and absorptive capabilities. Resilience is about the 'robustness' of systems. Organizations reach higher levels of resilience through purpose and relationships as cooperative strategies. They are able to reinvent themselves and find new business models that preserve the core. The way we set goals determines much of the relationship with stakeholders and the growth of the organization.

In this chapter, we have explored the capabilities that make up the enabling mode with the Performance Triangle and the Leadership Scorecard. We've demonstrated the agile capabilities that are needed to operate in the enabling mode.

THE ENABLING MODE

Enabling is the operations mode with agile capabilities for a dynamic environment. Agile demands an organization and management with leadership, systems and a culture that reconcile tensions, establishing an agile work environment for people to create value.

KEY CHAPTER IDEAS

- Enabling and controlling are ambidextrous capabilities
- Four levers come with five interactions, five tools and five enablers
- The Performance Triangle combines individual and organizational capabilities
- The Leadership Scorecard explains the management perspective of the triangle: Understand, think, act, enable and adhere
- The outcomes are speed, agility and resilience
- The test for agile capabilities at scale is success

ACTION AGENDA

With a design thinking mentality:
- Answer the Performance Triangle questions for all agile elements
- Answer the 20 questions on the Leadership Scorecard elements

If you get great answers, you likely have the elements for the enabling mode in place. If not, you should explore 'The People-Centric Shift' in Chapter 9.

FURTHER READING

Nold, H (2018). Dynamic Capabilities for People-Centric Management in Turbulent Times. *Dark Sides of Organizational Behavior and Leadership*. IntechOpen.

Michel, L (2013). *The Performance Triangle: Diagnostic Mentoring to Manage Organizations and People for Superior Performance in Turbulent Times*. London: LID Publishing.

Kotter, JP; and Heskett, JL (1992). *Corporate culture and performance*. New York: Free Press..

CHAPTER

THE PEOPLE-CENTRIC SHIFT

Imagine that you and your management team decided to make the shift to people-centric. You've agreed to adopt the people-centric principles. And now, you want to find out what it takes to make the shift, and to succeed with it.

Chapter 9 explains four shifts and the toolbox that is needed to make the shift to people-centric at scale. The shift requires work on the system. This means work on the Leadership Toolbox. We expand on the toolbox to suggest how you can make it agile in support of People-Centric Management.

A NEW PARADIGM

Figure 46 shows the shift from control to enabling as the people-centric paradigm shift.

FIGURE 46: THE PEOPLE-CENTRIC SHIFT

While control represents a stable platform with traditional managerial principles, enabling requires capabilities and tools with the ability to deal with a dynamic context. These people-centric principles are in sharp contrast to traditional leadership and systems. It's a paradigm shift to a conscious new management mindset, skill set and toolset.

A mindset shift usually means changing corporate culture. The new skill set requires leaders to learn new behaviours and decision-making styles. A new toolset requires an operating system that helps leaders enable good work rather than control. People-centric is here to stay. It is the adaptive manifestation of management in a dynamic era. The people-centric shift requires a holistic transformation of capabilities and the toolbox, not just a quick fix on tools.

The people-centric shift reconfigures resources that make a company different – those that are valuable, rare, inimitable and can't be substituted. In a dynamic environment, organizations need to constantly adapt their resource base. Agile capabilities offer the ability to select and use resources and competencies as processes that create, redefine, integrate, reconfigure and renew capabilities to achieve new outcomes, such as greater agility in a fast-changing environment.

But people-centric principles are not limited to a dynamic environment. The paradigm shift is about better exploiting existing capabilities and the exploration of new capabilities. The shift balances stability with agility.

A stable platform with traditional principles in support of exploitation cannot simultaneously be agile and constantly change to enable exploration. A strong focus on stability reduces agile forces. Stabilizing and destabilizing require different processes; one process cannot perform both. Applying and selecting the right tools is about stabilizing. On the other hand, observation and reflection facilitate the learning for a dynamic context. They enable organizations to create a dynamic toolbox. In combination, stabilizing control and enabling require a design with agile capabilities.

As such, the people-centric shift not only develops and applies agile capabilities and dynamic tools, but it deals with its inherent risks. It selects capabilities based on templates and patterns to solve the control problem, and it reduces the risks of dysfunctional viruses through early warning (e.g., self-reflection). With the people-centric shift, capabilities emerge through learning as a routine that frequently deals with change of capabilities and innovation. Design requires the selection of the right systems and a learning process for the development of these capabilities. It offers rules for change, learning mechanisms to accumulate experience, and ways to articulate and codify knowledge.

For managers, the challenge of the shift is to build the new capabilities and tools without losing control. A shift always requires a stable foundation, so making the shift successfully will require clarity on the starting point.

In a report titled, 'How to create an agile organization,' the global consulting powerhouse McKinsey (2017) argues that agile organizations excel at both stability and dynamism. Moreover, the report convincingly spotlights 18 dynamic practices that outperform stable practices in most aspects of strategy, process, structure, people and technology. Traditional organizations can improve performance by applying agile capabilities.

With a successful shift to people-centric principles, agile capabilities and a dynamic operating system, the new mindsets, skill sets and toolsets turn into an advantage. Such agile capabilities and dynamic systems are unique, and therefore difficult to copy. They are the foundations for a sustainable competitive advantage.

FOUR SHIFTS

The people-centric shift from control to enabling splits into four parts: the purpose, relationship, collaboration and learning shifts (Figure 47). Each part comes with a distinct mindset, skill set and toolset based on people-centric principles.

From	To	Levers	Shifts
Command	Self-responsibility	Know with clarity	1. The purpose shift
Power	Delegation	Move in one direction	2. The relationship shift
Bureaucracy	Self-organization	Mobilize the energy	3. The collaboration shift
Narrow targets	Attention	Maintain focus	4. The learning shift

FIGURE 47: FOUR SHIFTS

The purpose shift. The goal of the organization shifts from making money to delighting the customer. The role of the manager now is to help people find purpose, rather than telling them what do to.

The relationship shift. The relationship of individuals to their direct manager shifts to teams with delegated responsibility. And with that pivot, the role of the manager is to offer direction and enable a supportive work environment, not to check on people's work.

The collaboration shift. Instead of work being coordinated by bureaucracy with rules, plans and reports, it's coordinated through self-organization and agile approaches.

The learning shift. Rather than preoccupation with goals, efficiency and predictability, now, transparency, learning, sharing and continuous improvement help teams maintain their focus.

The four shifts require work *on* the system with the following questions:
1. How do we shift from command to self-responsible and know with clarity?
2. How do we shift from power to delegation and move in one direction?
3. How do we shift from bureaucracy to self-organization and mobilize energies?
4. How do we shift from narrow targets to wide direction and maintain focus?

The shift should start with storytelling, as it's a quick and inspirational way to make sense of what's happening to the wider team and organization. Rather than communicating and advocating the next change, you can establish credibility and trust by telling a story that touches lives. Storytelling translates abstract models and numbers into compelling images of the future.

THE PURPOSE SHIFT

The first shift is the story of people who know with clarity and find purpose. It's the shift from command to self-responsibility, with the goal of delighting the customer.

Command assumes that people need guidance to get things done. That guidance may range from detailed orders and control of actions to gentle observation. But both remain part of the traditional control mindset. It comes with traditional 'plan, do, check and act' management skills that are guided by extensive performance measurement and information tools.

In contrast, self-responsibility builds on motivation. By definition, self-responsible people are motivated by the ability to say no to things. They're driven by purpose that guides their engagement. By agreeing to get things done by their own will, they'll apply their creativity and knowledge to better deal with higher complexity.

The first shift (Figure 48) enables people to find purpose. It requires a different mindset, a new skill set and an enabling toolset that builds on distributed knowledge for a dynamic era.

Capabilities	Shift to	Purpose
Mindset	Self-responsibility	Motivation
Skill set	Interactive sense-making	Feedback and clarity
Toolset	Understanding	Create awareness, shared understanding

FIGURE 48: THE PURPOSE SHIFT

The shift from command to self-responsibility requires agile capabilities.

The shift of mind to self-responsibility. Self-responsibility is the prerequisite for motivation. It requires that leaders let go of traditional control modes. In a context where knowledge is widely distributed, agile assumes that people want to contribute and perform.

The shift to skills for feedback and sense-making. Motivated people demand purpose. They need feedback with information that helps them make sense. Agile demands active sense-making.

The shift of tools that deepen the understanding. Agile works with a toolbox that raises awareness of what matters most and creates a shared understanding.

Agility builds on a strong, stable foundation. And then, a successful shift to self-responsibility always builds on solid capabilities that enable people to know with clarity. The stability comes from skills and tools to assess market moves and performance indicators that offer reliable feedback. Without high quality diagnostic information, it's a risky shift and agility remains fragile.

THE RELATIONSHIP SHIFT

The second shift is for people to move in one direction and build relationships to enhance knowledge. It's a shift from power to delegated responsibility in teams.

Power originates from a mindset with an industrial background of low-skilled work, where people need to be told what to do. It implies hierarchy and concentrated knowledge at the top. Relationships are formed through pre-set structures and formal authority. Power is exercised in many shades of grey, and it's important to note that power and authority are neither bad nor good. There are times when power and authority are the only way to get things done fast.

Delegation assumes that knowledge is widely distributed and those who assume responsibility know what they are doing. Choice is left to those who assume delegated responsibility. The challenge comes from the need to move in one direction. Alignment with strategy must come from intense conversations and sharing, which establish productive relationships.

The relationship shift (Figure 49) enables people to build relationships. It requires a new set of conversation and interaction skills that help transcend the shared intent throughout the organization.

Capabilities	Shift to	Relationships
Mindset	Delegated authority in teams	Connectivity & sharing
Skill set	Interactive strategy conversation	Employer brand
Toolset	Thinking	Choice, shared intent

FIGURE 49: THE RELATIONSHIP SHIFT

The shift from power to delegation requires agile capabilities.

The shift of mind to delegation. Relationships at eye-level work with distributed power, where people are accountable for their actions. Agile capabilities ensure that people move in one direction. As such, delegation offers a new and superior kind of control.

The shift to skills for strategy conversations. Delegation requires connectivity, sharing and interaction. Agile capabilities, with conversations about strategy, enhance the employer brand and eventually employee loyalty.

The shift to tools that support the thinking. While traditional strategy tools focus on analysis, agile tools support delegated thinking throughout the organization. They offer choice and simultaneously enhance the bonding through a shared intent.

The shift from power to delegation does not mean that leaders lose control. Power is the stable platform from which the shift to delegation can be successfully made. Agile delegation demands interaction between leaders and employees on strategy and the way to get there.

THE COLLABORATION SHIFT

The third shift is of people who mobilize energy and collaborate across organizational boundaries. It's a shift from bureaucracy to coordination, and collaboration in self-organized teams.

Bureaucracy builds on efficiency with leaders, rules and routines to coordinate work. It works well with repetitive tasks that remain the same and where little collaboration is required. But we've also learned that trust is the fastest management concept around. Bureaucracy assumes a competitive environment where mistrust prevails. This is why there are alternatives to traditional bureaucracy.

Self-organization builds on natural trust and assumes that people at the client front are better equipped to coordinate where the work is being done. However, self-organization does not just happen. It requires energy from the outside, in the form of leadership. But that leadership differs from traditional control. It comes with tools that enable teams to properly function in an uncertain environment.

The collaboration shift (Figure 50) enables people to collaborate with a new set of skills and tools that creates trust and a shared agenda throughout the organization.

Capabilities	Shift to	Collaboration
Mindset	Self-organization	Resource flexibility
Skill set	Interactive performance conversation	Collaboration, value creation
Toolset	Delivery	Trust, shared agenda

FIGURE 50: THE COLLABORATION SHIFT

The shift from bureaucracy to self-organization requires agile capabilities.

The shift of mind to self-organization. It's a shift from fixed bureaucratic procedures to flexibility with resource allocation. Agile capabilities ensure that resources are available on demand.

The shift to skills for performance conversations. Interactions across organizational boundaries enhance collaboration. Agile, peer review-based conversations focus on value creation rather than goal achievement.

The shift to tools that focus on delivery. Traditional management-by-objectives systems are replaced by business plans and reviews owned by self-organized teams. Planning and reviews facilitate collaboration with a shared agenda, based on trust, and replace top-down bureaucracy.

The shift from bureaucracy to self-organization enables collaboration throughout the organization. Bureaucracy adds the stable platform with rigorous routines, while self-organizations provide the flexibility of combining resources. A successful shift builds on a stable platform.

THE LEARNING SHIFT

The fourth shift is the story of people who maintain the focus and learn. It's the shift from preoccupation with narrow targets to enabling teams to maintain their focus through learning, sharing and continuously improving.

Narrow targets limit the scope of action beyond team assignment or job descriptions. They're time-limited goals, set by managers to drive performance. Goals setting may range from fixed targets set by leaders to a contract that's agreed upon with employees. Yet, it remains a tool that cannot cope with higher volatility. The negative effects of gaming the target-setting process are widely discussed in the professional literature.

Attention with broad direction, in contrast, offers space and enables people to focus on things that matter most to their clients. Focus of attention, at the same time, is a tool that helps people learn and improve upon what they're doing.

The learning shift (Figure 51) enables people to focus attention and learn. It requires a different mindset, with new tools that work well in a volatile environment where knowledge dominates.

Capabilities	The Shift to	Learning
Mindset	Focus of attention	Accumulating knowledge
Skill set	Interactive contribution and risk dialogues	Entrepreneurial behaviours, decisions and actions
Toolset	Engagement and adherence	Focus, shared aspirations and norms

FIGURE 51: THE LEARNING SHIFT

The shift from narrow targets to attention based on broad direction requires people-centric capabilities.

The shift of mind to focus of attention. The primacy goes to seeing the whole rather than digging into all the detail. This is a shift away from goal setting with detailed, fixed targets; it's aimed at enabling people to focus attention within the frame of a broad direction.

The shift of skills to contribution and risk dialogues. These conversations zero in on how to maintain the focus rather than how to aim at goals. Focus directly impacts performance, whereas goals are an intellectual construct with no direct relationship to action.

The shift of tools to engage and adhere. Focus of attention enables learning. Agile tools establish the boundaries of the playing field, with beliefs and norms that frame entrepreneurial behaviours and actions. Broad direction and beliefs stretch the boundaries, whereas norms ensure that no one steps over the boundaries.

The learning shift changes leadership from applying detailed targets to communicating broad direction in support of entrepreneurial behaviours and actions. It assumes, however, that leaders have given some thought to the direction. A successful shift to people-centric builds on the stable platform that helps people maintain their focus and continuously learn.

THE LEADERSHIP TOOLBOX

The Leadership Toolbox (Figure 52) pulls together 20 tools that can help people understand, think, act, engage and adhere. The shift from traditional to people-centric calls for a new set of tools that support people performing and getting work done in a dynamic environment.

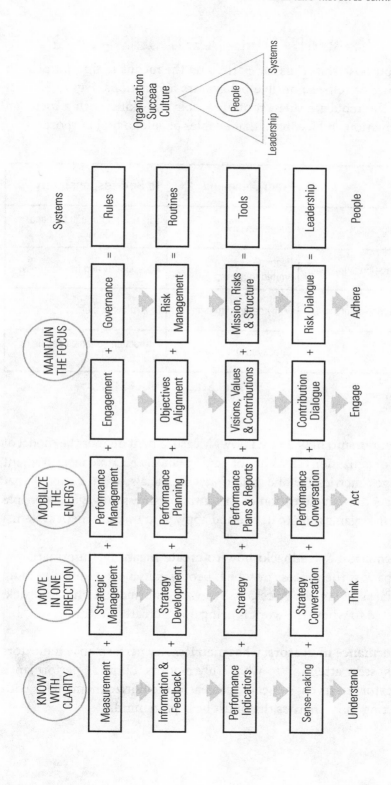

FIGURE 52: LEADERSHIP TOOLBOX

THE TOOLBOX FOR A DEEP UNDERSTANDING

The purpose shift calls for clarity and the means to find purpose in support of self-responsible behaviours and actions. Figure 53 outlines the requisite rules, routines, tools and skills, with a focus on information and feedback that enables people to find purpose.

	From Command	**To Self-responsibility**
Measurement	Budget review	Self-control through fast and frequent feedback
Information & feedback	Restrictive, limited to the top	Accessibility and transparency
Performance indicators	Many detailed metrics	Few relevant metrics
Sense-making	Directives and control	Interaction - enables people to find purpose

FIGURE 53: THE TOOLBOX TO UNDERSTAND

Measurement: how do we know? Measurement defines the model of how organizations think about performance. Dynamic measurement engages metrics beyond traditional financials, with a model that reflects the value creation of the entire business. Engage key people in your organization to define and apply your measurement system.

Information & feedback: how to create meaning? Information & feedback is the process by which people gain a deep understanding of what's going on. Access to relevant information and feedback, directed to where the work is being done, creates meaning.

Performance indicators: what metrics? Key performance indicators (KPIs) steer attention to what truly matters. Limiting performance indicators to seven, so people can easily memorize them, helps with selecting those metrics that must be kept in mind.

Sense-making: what's happening? Sense-making turns data into information and meaning for a better understanding of what's happening. It is the interaction mechanism that enables people to find purpose.

The purpose shift requires a new, dynamic toolbox that helps people understand what matters most.

THE TOOLBOX THAT ENABLES THINKING

The relationship shift calls for direction, and the means to relate and connect, in support of delegated authority. Figure 54 outlines the necessary rules, routines, tools and skills, with a focus on detailed analysis that helps people shift to thinking and searching for opportunities.

	From Power	**To Delegation**
Strategic management	Analysis	Modelling for super decision-making
Strategy development	Competitive analysis and advantage	Search for opportunities
Strategy	A 3-5-year plan	Value proposition, shared intent
Strategy conversation	Top-down messaging	Encouragement to take risks

FIGURE 54: THE TOOLBOX TO THINK

Strategic management: what direction? Strategic management refers to the approach organizations use to select their opportunities and challenges. Dynamic strategic management follows a model that enables delegated structured thinking. It establishes a shared language for how people think about their business and enables them to define and articulate strategy.

Strategy development: how to create the strategy? Strategy development guides the thinking. Dynamic strategy development is about innovation and new opportunities. Make it a continuous process that engages key people, not simply the topic of a once-a-year off-site executive meeting. Rather than cascading strategy downward, enable delegated decision-making in teams, allowing them to create their strategies.

Strategy: what direction? In simplest terms, strategy defines the value that the business promises to its stakeholders, starting with clients, employees, suppliers, the public and shareholders. The brand of the business attaches specific values to its promises. This is why a dynamic strategy establishes a strong relationship with people and a shared intent to move in one direction.

Strategy conversation: why are we going there? Strategy conversation helps leaders establish direction. It's part of the daily routine to create shared intent. It is effective when it enables people to think, rather than providing them with a posted message.

The relationship shift requires a new, dynamic toolbox that enables people to make decisions in line with the intent. The toolbox works when the collective thinking results in opportunities as true innovations.

THE TOOLBOX THAT FOCUSES ON DELIVERY

The collaboration shift calls for delivery and the means to collaborate in support of self-organization. Figure 55 outlines the relevant rules, routines, tools and skills, with a focus on budgets and shifting to engagement to create value.

	From Bureaucracy	**To Self-organization**
Performance management	Fixed budgets	Planning as a continuous and engaging process
Performance planning	Annual top-down budgeting	Just-in-time resource availability, rigorous (peer) performance reviews
Performance plans and reports	Fixed annual budgets	Relative goals
Performance conversation	Business planning	Interactive, dynamic coordination

FIGURE 55: THE TOOLBOX TO DELIVER

Performance management: what is our model? The main purpose of performance management is to implement the strategy. Self-organization demands a model that enables teams to manage their own performance. In a dynamic context, continuous planning and review based on relative goals beats traditional top-down budgeting.

Performance planning and business reviews: how to implement? In a dynamic context, strategy (the thinking) and implementation (the doing) are not separated. They are one continuous process that links hierarchical levels and seamlessly coordinates with related departments. Dynamic planning and review are by no means out of control. On the contrary, they enable peer-control through rigorous business reviews.

Performance plans and reports: what goals and steps? Dynamic plans and reports focus on action, not on financial projections. Rather than detailed targets, relative goals and actions are documented and reviewed regularly, based on two-page documents.

Performance conversation: are we on track, and what can we do?
People-centric demands more interaction and less paper. As such, performance conversations facilitate resource allocation, action planning and performance reviews. These conversations have one goal: how to mobilize the right and sufficient resources to implement strategy collaboratively, as a team.

In simplest terms, planning is a mature conversation between the leader who demands the value and a leader who delivers it. It's a commitment and a contract between the two. And yes, this is accompanied by a process for how to get there. More important than the actual content of that contract is the conversation about concerns with the plan. Knowing about the concerns takes the fear out of the alignment with your leader.

A business review is an after-action review. It is good practice to have that facilitated by someone who is not part of the delivery and performance dynamic. A good business review is one where you can come in as the leader at the end and share your reflections – what have we learned from this? Capture and document business reviews, to feed and inform the next cycle or situation.

The collaboration shift requires a new, dynamic toolbox that uses the motivation of people to deliver performance in teams. The toolbox works well when teams apply their knowledge and energy to things they care about.

THE TOOLBOX THAT FRAMES ENGAGEMENT AND ADHERENCE

The learning shift calls for engagement and adherence, and the means to learn in support of broad direction. Figure 56 outlines the pertinent rules, routines, tools and skills – with a focus on targets and incentives – in the shift to enabling people to learn and act as entrepreneurs.

	From Targets	**To Focus of Attention**
Engagement, governance	Performance targets, rules, and incentives	Shared values, social control, entrepreneurship
Objectives alignment, risk management	Incentives for plan achievement	Trust teams on self-control
Vision, values, mission, risks, structures	Narrow hierarchies with wordy directives	Base accountability on holistic factors
Contribution and risk dialogues	Control	Learning

FIGURE 56: THE TOOLBOX TO ENGAGE AND ADHERE

Engagement: how to get the mileage? Traditional engagement models focus on performance targets and incentive plans. Dynamic engagement systems are based on motivated people who want to deliver performance. Performance targets and rewards are applied at team or unit levels, rather than to individuals.

Governance: how to set the rules? In a dynamic environment, governance rules are defined as principles rather than strict operating procedures, to allow for entrepreneurial action rather than adherence to rules. Social control replaces management action.

Objectives alignment: how to coordinate? In a hierarchical setting with performance targets and incentives, the hierarchical cascading of objectives takes considerable management time. People-centric demands the alignment of goals among departments that need to work together. In that way, objectives become the means to coordinate and align to the firm's goals.

Risk management: how to avoid the undesired? Risk management is often seen as a once-a-year executive assessment of the company's overall risks. In a dynamic context, risks are assessed continuously. It's a learning process that attempts to see the invisible and raise awareness of the organization's boundaries.

Vision, values and contributions: what expectations? Ambitions work like magnets; they create effortless pull. Vision and values are important sources of energy. They help people focus their attention on what truly matters – their contributions.

Mission, risks and structures: what rules? Dynamic boundaries frame what is inside and what is outside the limits of the business. They help people limit their activities to the set boundaries without limiting entrepreneurship.

Contribution dialogue: what do you need? The contribution dialogue is an ongoing interaction with leaders on what's needed to succeed and how we can still achieve our goals. Leaders help employees maintain their focus on the overall goals of the business.

Risk dialogue: where are the boundaries? The risk dialogue sets the boundaries for entrepreneurial action. Leaders are in a dialogue with people on what decisions and actions are within and outside the boundaries of the business.

The learning shift requires a new, dynamic toolbox that focuses attention and limits distractions. The toolbox works well when people are encouraged to balance efficiency and entrepreneurship. It supports continuous learning rather than control.

So far in this chapter, we have reviewed four concurrent shifts from traditional to people-centric. We've also expanded on agile capabilities and the new, dynamic toolbox that is needed to make it a paradigm shift. But, be wary of *fake agile*.

WATCH OUT FOR FAKE AGILE

With the rise and success of agile, fake agile has become a concern and badly-done agile has grown. It comes from leaders who are afraid of letting bureaucracy go and coaches who promote all sorts of dubious methodologies under the umbrella of agile.

Agile is not a fix for every problem. It is a capability that helps organizations better deal with the challenges of a dynamic market context. The gap between the 10% of firms that are truly agile and the 90% that want to be is filled with companies that claim to be agile.

Here are four questions that can help determine just how genuine your agile is:

1. Is the main purpose of your organization to create a customer? Does anyone know that with clarity?
2. Do you delegate relevant decisions to teams at the client front, and connect them? Do you help them move in the same direction?
3. Do you coordinate work through self-organization? Do you allocate resources on demand?
4. Do you enable the organization to maintain the focus of attention through broad direction? Does this enable learning?

If your answers to all of these questions is yes, you have developed genuine agility. If the answers are no, you need to focus on beating fake agile.

In this chapter we have explored four concurrent shifts, with a new toolbox that facilitates the shift at scale and enables People-Centric Management. Twenty tools align the Leadership Toolbox with the enabling operating mode.

The next chapter outlines what real people-centric looks like.

THE PEOPLE-CENTRIC SHIFT

The people-centric shift changes the paradigm of how we manage and organize.

KEY CHAPTER IDEAS

- People-centric needs design; it's a paradigm shift from controlling to enabling people with a new mindset, skill set and toolset
- Four shifts make it happen: purpose, relationship, collaboration and learning
- The Leadership Toolbox offers 20 tools for the people-centric way

ACTION AGENDA

Find out whether your people-centric needs a shift:
- Identify changes in your context
- Identify interferences and unused potential
- Identify your current and future operating mode
- Determine your future Leadership Toolbox

FURTHER READING

Nold, H; and Michel, L (2016). The Performance Triangle: A Model for Corporate Agility. *Leadership & Organization Development, Journal*, Vol. 37 No. 3.

Denning, S. How to Make the Whole Organization Agile, *Forbes*, 22. July 2015.

Pfeffer, J; and Sutton, RI (2000). *The Knowing-Doing Gap: How Smart Companies Turn Knowledge into Action.* Boston, Harvard Business School Press.

Hamel, G (2000). *Leading the Revolution.* Boston, Harvard Business School Press.

CHAPTER

10

THE DUAL OPERATING SYSTEM

So far, I have made the case for people-centric, agile, dynamic and the enabling mode as if that was the only choice. In most organizations, hybrid contexts and modes, infused with elements of both traditional and people-centric, coexist or depend on each other. People-centric needs stability, and traditional needs to put people back into their organizations.

We will now explore how People-Centric Management functions as the bridge that brings together different modes as dual operating systems. Dual refers to the coexistence of two or more operating systems.

This chapter outlines the features of an operating system that balances effectiveness and innovation with a toolbox that brings out the advantages of both traditional and people-centric. First, we'll look at the features of control, engaging, change and enabling operating systems. Second, we'll discuss why this is not sufficient. Third, we'll explore dual operating systems and expand on how to scale and simultaneously individualize them to fit the specific needs of people and organizations.

In previous chapters, the focus was on people-centric, agile and dynamic capabilities and the enabling mode for three reasons. First, traditional management is known to most of us as it is documented in books, taught at business schools and practiced in organizations. There is no need to duplicate that. Second, people-centric, agile dynamic management is new, with less of a theoretical backing in management science. Agile emerged and was applied in isolated areas of IT rather than corporate-wide. Third, the context for most organizations has shifted from a relatively stable environment to one that is dynamic.

Agile is the dynamic capability that most organizations are still in the process of developing. Dynamic is a deliberate choice. Having that choice is also new for most organizations and leaders. We have explored the alternatives as people-centric.

FOUR OPERATING SYSTEMS

Domestication is a distinctive feature of operating systems and, at the same time, a barrier to changing operating systems. Domestication translates explicit systems into implicit values, capabilities and behaviours as deeply embedded in culture. Culture works like glue. This makes it hard to reconfigure operating systems.

It won't come as a surprise that managers and employees are expected to make quick decisions, focus their actions on what matters most and demonstrate entrepreneurial behaviours in everything they do.

Reality strikes, and offers something even more startling. In the context of our information-rich, dynamic environment, the requirements and expectations outlined above are virtually impossible to meet – people are distracted, struggle with decisions and miss opportunities. As such, managers and employees often have no choice but to act in a self-interested manner. As a consequence, talent is not effectively used and companies perform far below their potential. This challenge is endemic in the dynamic and knowledge-driven environment, in which we have become comfortably uncomfortable.

Systematic information overload, analysis paralysis, endless meetings, bias towards rationality, risk aversion and blindly following rules dominate our ways of thinking and doing at work. This comes at the expense of disciplined decision-making, deliberate actions and behaviours aligned with company beliefs and boundaries. We know that this is the result of strong domestication.

In a virus-infected culture, faulty leadership and erroneous managerial systems lead to flawed decisions, missing action and undesired behaviours. The negative domestication spiral accelerates because of this deteriorating operating environment. Domestication is what we define as the behaviours and actions whereby leaders and employees follow the habits and patterns determined by the organization's rules, norms and values.

On the positive side, a vibrant culture, interactive leadership and supportive systems enable fast decisions, actions with impact and the desired behaviours. These are the outcomes of an operating system with a deliberate design, leading to positively domesticated behaviours: these companies enable a high degree of individual effectiveness, where the talent is effectively used.

People follow given rules. They want to do good. That's why the operating system is so important. It domesticates how people decide, act and behave. It is deeply embedded in the organization's culture. With this comes the challenge of responding when the operating system requires change. Changing operating systems influences the rules, routines and tools people follow. Taking all of that into account, how can organizations jump-start positive domestication?

The idea of positive socialization starts with every individual's return on management (ROM). Harvard Business School Professor Robert Simons developed the concept in 1995, based on the fact that time, attention and energy are scarce resources for any human being. In order to achieve a high ROM, it's wise to carefully invest time and focus attention to generate a maximum amount of productive energy. We know that many leaders and employees struggle with this.

> **ROM = PRODUCTIVE ENERGY RELEASED / TIME AND ATTENTION INVESTED**

An operating system must yield a high ROM (Figure 57). It supports individual effectiveness, time, attention, energy and organizational effectiveness through efficiency, innovation and value creation.

Effectiveness	Exploitation	Exploration	Outcome
Individual	Time	Attention	Energy
Organizational	Efficiency	Innovation	Value creation

FIGURE 57: RETURN ON MANAGEMENT

Figure 58 positions four operating systems in line with the operating modes: control, engagement, change and enabling. Each has a different purpose and outcome that spans traditional and people-centric.

Managers choose and mix four operating systems, depending on the specific managerial context in which their organizations operate.

FIGURE 58: FOUR OPERATING SYSTEMS

I've argued that the changing environment and a tech-savvy generation's knowledge and talents force companies to be clear about the operating mode.

Four questions help us distinguish the four operating modes:
1. How do we engage people and know with clarity?
2. How do we make superior decisions and move in one direction?
3. How do we coordinate work and mobilize the energy?
4. How do we enable performance and maintain the focus?

Enabling operating systems comprise self-responsible, decisive collective decisions with a focus on learning and development. In control operating systems, decisions are deferred to senior management with power at the top of the hierarchy. Engagement systems facilitate collective debate and motivation, whereas with change systems, management takes corrective action. Figure 59 summarizes the features of the four operating systems.

Operation	Control	Change	Engagement	Enabling
Systems	Hierarchy and power	Management action	Individual knowledge	Learning and development
Context	Comparably stable environment	High uncertainty and pace	Knowledge and technology intensive	High complexity and ambiguity
How we understand and engage	Leaders motivate, extrinsic rewards	Stretched goals and incentives	Mastery and meaning	Self-responsibility and purpose
How we think and decide	Through hierarchy	By leaders	Debate and reason	Collective wisdom
How we act and coordinate	Processes and operating procedures	Change projects	Workshops and meetings	Self-organization, mutual adjustment
How we behave and motivate	Top-down goals and control	Aligned action	Self-interest	Wide goals, shared mindset

FIGURE 59: FEATURES OF OPERATING SYSTEMS

Operating systems come with a toolbox for leaders and employees that helps them use time effectively, focus attention and mobilize the productive energy.

The dominant operating system varies depending on the business context in which a company operates. More often than not, companies unwillingly and unknowingly operate with mixed (or multiple) operating systems that vary within the organization. And, my research confirms that 45% of companies still operate in the control-based operating mode.

For example, a global pharmaceutical industry company I worked with used the engagement mode for its research and development function, while the manufacturing part applied the control-based system. The selection and design of the toolbox for each mode of operations is a senior executive task that requires experience.

In a highly regulated, safety-first context, the control-based operating systems may still be effective. Change-based operating systems are the norm in transaction-oriented and heavily technology-supported industries, such as insurance, banking and telecom. Engagement-based operating systems do well in knowledge-driven environments, such as educational institutions or professional-services businesses.

Counter-intuitively, operating systems can be observed in a variety of settings that require both a high degree of flexibility and a rigorous set of operating procedures. This is certainly the case in the work of a commercial airline pilot, the emergency room of a hospital, in a military in combat situation, or in a firefighting situation. These examples do not illustrate normal, everyday business operations, but looking at the extremes helps to make the point.

Nobody would ever go into a restaurant kitchen and ask for the specifics of a recipe before ordering a meal. It is expected that the chef knows what he's doing.

In an emergency room, we trust the exceptional skills of highly trained doctors, nurses and technicians who intuitively do what is right in the specific situation and context. They're trained to follow strict standards, but when the situation requires, it is their skills rather than the routines that save lives. Agility and capabilities beat rigorous routines.

In military combat or a firefighting situation, leaders can only provide broad guidance on how to go about handling a specific emergency. At the battlefront or the scene of a fire, well-developed skills and intuition are required to do what is necessary. No command from above could ever be better at reacting quickly and flexibly to fit the situation. Soldiers and firefighters respond in the best way their intuition and trained behaviours allow; they have absorbed rigorous procedures on how to deal with emergencies and simultaneously create resilient states.

Well-developed operating systems facilitate intuitive decision-making (the agile elements) and trained routine (the stable elements) rather than authority, blind action and decisions by paralysis. And so, they allow for fast responses, permit flexible action and enable robust solutions.

ENGAGING SELF-RESPONSIBLE PEOPLE

The control-based operating system is what most of us know well. For the past 100 years, industrial-style leaders have been trained to motivate and control people. Moreover, despite the wealth of research proving that there's no meaningful relationship between bonuses and performance, extensive extrinsic and monetary rewards continue to dominate people management. Stretched goals tied to incentives are the predominant means of control-based operating systems.

The fact is that control-based systems achieve exactly what they're intended to: fulfilment of detailed objectives, and not one bit more. As management thinker Peter Drucker once said: "Management by objectives works – if you know the objectives. Ninety percent of the time you don't." The engagement-based operating system demands personal mastery and meaning to engage people. We know from the philosophers of 17th century European Humanism that self-responsible people are by definition motivated people.

The engagement-based operating system is built on the assumption that people are fundamentally motivated and, as such, the management task is to help employees find that purpose. This is called sense-making, not sense-giving.

High-performance sports professionals around the world know that engaged people need four things to perform at their peak:

1. They must be able to focus their attention on what matters most to them
2. They need a high degree of awareness of what's most important
3. They trust their own skills and their environment
4. They require choice

Choice is a prerequisite for self-responsible behaviours. If you cannot say no, then you have no choice, and therefore cannot be self-responsible. Managers are well advised to give this some careful thought.

As an example, a renowned leadership think tank I worked with decided to invest in 'people engagement' activities, as recommended by mainstream consultants. No doubt, their efforts resulted in a better place to work. But the company lost on speed, agility and robustness. Meetings, town halls and more personal conversations augmented the sense of purpose, but what truly mattered to the organization was whether employees could fully apply their talent and focus on priorities to get things done.

Insights from the Diagnostic revealed the need to complement engagement activities with a toolbox for 21st century working practices. Less than two months after these practices were put in place at the organization, creativity increased, collaboration became a natural way of working, and relevant knowledge was shared and accumulated.

Self-responsible action and a deep sense of purpose enable people to use their time most effectively. As a result, their organizations get things done faster, and still have things under control, despite a more dynamic environment.

MAKING DECISIONS BASED ON COLLECTIVE WISDOM

With control-based operating systems, decisions are made through hierarchy. Delegated decisions always require the manager's signature, which means the boss always makes the decisions. We know that most leaders understand that this type of hierarchy makes organizations slow, inflexible and fragile.

In change-based operations, it's always the leader who decides, assuming that they're the most qualified and most knowledgeable in the organization. As the author Henry Mintzberg would put it: In these organizations, people are seen as re(movable) human resources, costly human assets and human capital. They aren't seen as human beings who add value to an organization.

In contrast, engagement-based operations favour debate, reasoning and committees. People are valued for what they add: knowledge and experience. It's just that filling calendars with endless meetings doesn't add to the agility of these companies.

Enabling operations favour decision-making through collective wisdom. Decisions are delegated to the most knowledgeable and skilled person. Rapid feedback ensures that individuals and organizations learn quickly, and continuously improve their decision-making and implementation of these decisions.

A high-tech utilities provider I work with successfully transformed from a CEO-driven, decision-making style to a collective approach. The challenges of the energy sector – with decreasing investment in traditional energy sources and more in riskier new sources – demands that companies continuously sense what is politically acceptable, judge what is possible and decide what is doable. As such, energy companies require ongoing sensing and debate, without 'losing it' to analysis by paralysis.

With the help of the Diagnostic, the CEO of this particular company was able to change his approach and began to mobilize knowledge and insights from his executive team. This quickly transformed his team into a body that used its collective wisdom and made the entire company more people-centric, without it getting locked in decisions without choices.

COORDINATING SELF-ORGANIZED WORK

With control-based operating systems, the coordination of work happens through detailed processes. Every time naturally-connected parts fall apart, these companies install further operating procedures.

With the change-based operating system, managers initiate change projects to reconnect parts that have become disconnected through recently-added structures and accountabilities. Workshops, meetings, alignment and role clarifications are believed to be the means to coordinate work with the engagement-based operating system.

The enabling-based operating system supports companies with decentralized businesses. Self-organized teamwork and ad-hoc project teams are favoured over strictly following plans and budgets.

Pharmaceutical industry firms I work with have long-established project teams that develop assets from research, development, distribution, marketing and sales as parts of their business. Functions allocate knowledge and experience throughout the course of flexible and temporary projects. People mutually adjust in a self-organized and purpose-driven manner to release their productive energy. In this way, they help their organization remain flexibly grounded in a stable backbone.

Self-organized work and mutual adjustment helps employees focus their attention on what matters most. A high degree of agility comes from the fact that shifting focus within a shared purpose makes organizations flexible.

THRIVING PERFORMANCE THROUGH BROAD PURPOSE

Control-based operating systems apply rigorous individual management by objectives with top-down goals and frequent performance appraisals. People in these modes spend a lot of time getting agreement on and conducting reviews of the performance objectives.

Change-based operations favour action orientation. In other words, valuable management time is dedicated to aligning value-adding projects and coordinating actions. These companies argue that implementation is what makes or breaks performance.

In engagement-based organizations, knowledge-driven employees follow their self-interest, making it difficult for management to get in balance with corporate intent.

People working in enabling-based systems support teams with a shared mindset and clarity, based on broad direction, with a strong, shared purpose. Managers help them understand and use their energy to apply their full talent.

A public transportation company we recently worked with had transformed from government agency to independent entrepreneurial unit. One of the legacies it brought along was the rigid management by objectives system that dominated most management conversations. It was good practice to be very detailed and concrete when it came to target setting. A review of the organization's Leadership Toolbox with the Diagnostic revealed that rigorous and detailed routines made the entire company slow, inflexible and fragile, like every other bureaucratic public administration.

By focusing people on 'serving their clients' – offering the city population the world's best public transportation system – it unlocked the energy of its talent. This led to an entrepreneurially-driven organization that was no longer weighed down by the negative effects of detailed targets.

Organizations with enabling-based systems are able to release their productive energies based on a broad sense of purpose, cooperation and high connectivity. These are the features of highly resilient businesses.

WHY WE ARE
WHERE WE ARE

Levers describe traditional and People-Centric Management. Traditional management is associated with efficiency, and with command and control, power, bureaucracy and narrow targets. Existing resources are used to create competitive advantage and deliver shareholder returns. Its implicit design is to exploit resources to maximize value. People-centric and agile are at the other end of the lever. People-centric relates to creativity that demands self-responsibility, delegation, self-organization and attention. Agile is designed for exploration, innovation and finding new ways of doing things to create new value.

Both efficiency and innovation are part of every organization. Efficiency without the growth of innovative new products is not sustainable. Similarly, just being innovative without consistently delivering value to clients is not an option. Most organizations want a hybrid – the benefits of both traditional and People-Centric Management, in their own specific mix. Traditional management adds stability to agile. Agile brings cooperation back into traditional management. The specific mix and the dual features come from a dynamic operating system with a design based on people-centric principles.

A bit of history helps us understand why we need to care about people. The management writer and teacher David Hurst (2014, 2018) put it as follows:

Traditional management is deeply embedded in the Anglo-American management mindset. This mindset is practiced as what the Harvard Business School's Chris Argyris called 'theory-in-use.' It is not the philosophical views that are expressed when you speak to managers. This predominant 'Cartesian' view – derived from the teachings of philosopher René Descartes – sees management as an engineering-like applied science, where the conscious mind and the actor (manager) are detached. His role is to rationally analyse, decide and give practical instructions.

Many of the traditional management 'innovations' of the past failed because of this predominant mindset. It assumes and transcends an impoverished and inadequate view of humankind. The scholar and educator Sumantra Ghoshal (2008) called it the negative assumptions that underlie traditional management.

Humans don't have one dominant mind. We have two minds that work together and play the inner game. In line with Gallwey's (2000) concept of the inner game, Self 1 is about the rational mind that makes judgments, gives commands and takes action. Self 2 is the human being himself, with all his potential and experience. Peak performance happens when Self 1 is quiet and Self 2 is in the flow. Nothing interferes with the potential.

Similarly, the psychologist and economist Daniel Kahnemann (2011) calls them System 1 and System 2. As he described it, System 1 is fast, automatic, active and unconscious. System 2 is slow, tiring, aware and logical.

The traditional 'division of the mind' offers left and right hemispheres. The left-brain deals with the familiar, predictable, known, fixed, static, decontextualized and explicit. The right-brain is concerned with the novel, the possible, the unknown, variability, dynamics, the embedded and the implicit.

Philosophy suggests that the first brain (The Master) is existential. It handles questions like, 'Who am I?' and 'Why do I matter?' The second brain (His Emissary) is instrumental in dealing with questions like, 'What do I want?' and 'How do I get it?' Central to one's real-world functioning is the relationship between the 'we' and the 'I' – the collective and the individual, soft and hard – which allows us to collaborate and to compete.

The prevailing scientific managerial mindset focuses on the rational, the known, the executive 'I' in pursuit of efficiency. As a result, people are treated as a means rather than an end. In that mindset, management innovations need to appeal to efficiency. This makes approaches with a focus on experience, awareness, the unknown and the 'we' hard to sell. And, we get more of the same efficiency – linear, mechanical, process-oriented.

The Cartesian view works well in the context of natural sciences. In management, its use is limited to a predictable context, when simple steps work, and where cause-and-effect relationships are stable. Such systems are simple. Rules and processes work well in that kind of a context.

However, the Cartesian mindset does not work when it is applied to complex and dynamic systems where parameters are unstable, agents are interdependent, and cause-and-effect is non-linear. There is no manual for that. Dynamic contexts require an organic, ecological, adaptive approach. Things emerge, develop, and are nurtured and cultivated. It may be true that no two situations are the same, but history matters. And, experience is what puts things into habit.

People-centric has emerged from a different history, with a different mindset. It's a mindset that is closely related to the humanist view of the world. Ghoshal (2008), who we cited earlier regarding negative assumptions, would summarize this ethos as the set of positive assumptions that make up agile management.

Again, another brief walk through history helps. The ancient Greeks introduced the concept of 'here and now' – the conviction that the past keeps humans from being happy, as it includes nostalgia, guilt and pangs of conscience. The notion of *the here and now* centres between memories of the past and plans for the future. It provides us with wellbeing and freedom. And, it means that people are better off accepting the current reality.

Aristotle, the so-called 'Father of Western Philosophy,' used the term *phronesis* to describe practical wisdom, and *techne* for technical expertise. In *techne,* end-goals are set in advance and reason applied to determine the best mean to achieve them. With *phronesis,* ends and means are entangled. It requires experience, knowledge and situational judgment to understand the context and formulate decisions about what is right. *Techne* can be learned, while *phronesis* can only be gained through experience.

The Reformation, with Martin Luther, Huldrych Zwingli and Johannes Calvin, and the Humanism that followed, introduced a new image of mankind. Humans are self-sufficient, meaning they can act and decide without the guidance of the cosmos or a god. They have the capacity to think and learn – the desire and ability to perfect themselves. And humans are free to decide. This is the foundation of the modern society and, I would suggest, of management.

Modern morale is the consequence of individual freedom, the benefits of goodwill and care about common wealth. Egoism is evident in people who have no difficulty knowing what needs to be done, but allow themselves exceptions every now and then. But freedom ends at the boundary of where the freedom of others starts. The Humanistic psychology advanced by Abraham Maslow and Carl Rogers emphasized that human personality develops with the goal of personal fulfilment.

The philosopher Kant saw people in the world of free will as 'purpose' and not as a 'means.' He characterized them as possessing dignity that may not be used to achieve higher goals. His work redefined the role of work as the task to create the world, to change, and to improve things based on goodwill.

Values are the foundation of every society. Yet, they don't give human existence sufficient purpose, goals or direction. The political philosopher Jean-Jacques Rousseau argued that we cannot live without freedom, values and purpose. But that's not the same as saying that we use them. The philosopher Georg WF Hegel expanded on learning, saying: "Experience is to leave ourselves in order to find ourselves again."

Humanist management thinking that favours teaming and collaboration through respect for people had its history too. Its proponents have included the theorists Mary Parker Follett (1920s), Elton Mayo and Chester Barnard (1930s), Abraham Maslow (1940s), Douglas McGregor (1960s), Peter Drucker (1970s), Tom Peters and Robert Waterman (1980s), Jon Katzenbach and Douglas Smith (1990s), and Gary Hamel (2000s).

This formed the mindset and tradition that is deeply embedded in many European SME's, which have practiced agile for the last 100 years, without naming or even being aware of it. Yet, despite almost a century of distinguished management writing, the truth is that the concept did not have a lasting impact on general management practice.

People-centric builds on a positive humanist tradition: Current reality helps people focus attention. Choice is freedom. Purpose is motivation. People are self-responsible.

People-centric needs to be experienced. Only then can the learning that the inner game promotes be translated into action. I truly believe that managers should research, learn more about and embrace elements of the Reformation and Humanism, to better understand the ways of thinking needed to grasp agility. Unfortunately, as mired as they are in the Cartesian mindset, it's unlikely that many will make that shift without a change in identity, and existential change in the way of looking at the self.

But, there's hope. In recent years, with Nobel prizes being awarded to the scientists and economists associated with the discipline, behavioural economics has been 'discovered.' Kahnemann was awarded the prize in 2002 for integrating psychology into economics when people make decisions under uncertainty. In 2013, Robert J Shiller received the award for his work on asset pricing through behavioural finance. And, in 2017, Robert Thaler received a Nobel Prize for establishing that people are irrational in ways that defy economic theory.

Homo economicus, the rational human decision-maker who acts in his own interest, is being fundamentally questioned.

Along the way, the humanist movement has gotten help from the internet by shifting power in the marketplace from the seller to the buyer. Customers with access to information, choice and the ability to interact with each other now collectively have much more power. The need to innovate with people to become better, cheaper, faster, smaller, more convenient and more individual is the norm. This means that organizations need to turn to employees with talent and a passion for work to find new and better ways to serve customers.

Today, competitive advantage is determined by interactions and relationships with customers and based on motivated, talented and skilful people. The strategies of the traditional model, with its myopic focus on growth and profitability, are replaced by 'Why do customers buy from us?' and 'What else might they want?'

Traditional bureaucracy simply can't get this job done. Enabling, people-centric, agile and dynamic models are well suited to it. With the goal of delighting customers, managers don't need to motivate employees to do the job. With managers and employees sharing the same goal – creating a customer – the humanistic, agile practices of awareness, choice, trust and focus become not only possible but downright necessary.

People-centric, agile and dynamic capabilities have the potential to return management to what it should have always been: the ends.

OPERATING IN
A DUAL MODE

Now, let's turn to the dual operating system. As explained earlier, the operating system of an organization is made of systems, leadership and culture. Management can design systems and promote leadership interactions. Culture is an outcome of supportive systems and good leadership.

I have associated culture with mindset. Now, to expand on the operating system, the focus is on the toolbox – the rules, routines, tools and skill set of leaders. A dual operating system combines traditional and people-centric in a way that helps organizations manage in hybrid contexts. It hinges on the ability to manage as the context changes, without the interferences of traditional approaches, such as change- and performance-management.

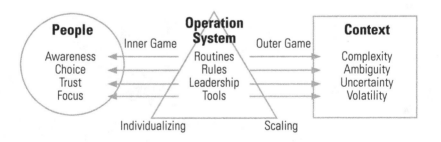

FIGURE 60: THE DUAL OPERATING SYSTEM

The dual operating systems (Figure 60) enable people to 'play the inner game' and, simultaneously, 'play their outer game.' The inner game is what happens with people between the ears. It's how they deal with distorting thoughts. The outer game refers to how people and the organization at large address the challenges of the context in which they operate and how they capture business opportunities.

The dual features of the operating systems come from the need to support people in applying their knowledge and skills with their inner game, and the organization as a whole with its outer game. The inner game offers the capacity for people to be agile, unlock their creativity and perform at their peak. The outer brings about the reliability, consistency and reproducibility that are expected from an efficient organization.

A dual operating system meets a number of important criteria.

To cope with growing complexity, routines need to create awareness rather than control. Complexity is like water; it cannot be compacted. Better awareness is the only way to deal with increased complexity. Traditional ways of addressing complexity include deconstructing it, setting goals and delegating decision-making. Increased complexity is a frequent cause of ineffective, bureaucratic routines and managerial processes. The fix for this is appropriate design that re-establishes the missing rigour. One can prevent an emphasis on control by designing routines that enable higher levels of awareness.

In times of increasing ambiguity, rules must enable choice. When the future is unclear, choice in decision-making performs better than standard operating procedures. Greater ambiguity is a frequent cause of 'infected' rules and the lack of discipline to follow them. Agility and speed in dealing with ambiguities requires a design for choice.

To cope with rising levels of uncertainty, a leader needs to trust rather than command. The only way to deal with uncertainty is to trust in your own capabilities. With increasing uncertainty, it is important to define a management policy that balances responsibility and outside control. The fix for flawed leadership is to design interactions better, to improve relationships and support collaboration. To prevent creeping uncertainty from hampering performance, interactions require a design with features that enable trust.

To address greater volatility, tools must focus attention rather than aim. When things change quickly, people need something they can hold on to. Use tools that focus attention on what is important. With increasing volatility and market dynamics, it's important to get the control policy right, as a balance between enabling self-initiative and fostering goal achievement. The way to fix erroneous tools is to redesign for purpose and collaboration. Prevent focus on the wrong things by using tools that help people focus their attention rather than just enabling control.

Knowledge people want choice, awareness, the ability to focus their attention and trust. The same agile features of an operating system that is built for a dynamic environment are required in the context where knowledge work dominates. As such, a dynamic operating system features everything that's needed to operate in a dual mode, in a stable and a dynamic environment.

One of the fathers of scientific management, the French engineer and mining executive Henri Fayol, identified the need to plan, organize, command, coordinate and control in his role as a manager. Management by objectives followed, to strengthen control and alignment. Detailed budgets and performance targets became the tools that offered predictability, suggesting that the future was mapped out. Later, strategic planning was added, with better ways of modelling to predicting the future.

Today, planning is challenged as the cycles of change have become shorter than what planning was intended to handle. Executives are wary of traditional planning, as it feels like a duty, and is slow and cumbersome. Yet, planning is essential for every organization if we care about people and resources. Dynamic planning is decentralized, follows short cycles, is continuous, and favours flexible goals. Such planning systems have a design that facilitates interactive leadership. This facilitates coordination and alignment, and combines big data and judgment. Dynamic adds to the tradition of planning; with a design for people, it merges flexibility and stability.

SCALING AND INDIVIDUALIZING MANAGEMENT

Scaling and individualizing the operating system prepares management for hybrid modes, with the dual features of enabling dynamic features while offering stability and efficiency. People-centric is the feature that combines scaling and individualizing.

In Chapter 1, on the new business context, we distinguished between a stable environment and a dynamic one. A hybrid context exists when organizations experience stable and dynamic events, or operate in parts that are stable and dynamic. A hybrid context also exists when events or parts of the organization require control and others demand agile responses at the same time. Managers have a choice. They can operate on two different modes with two operating systems, or they can operate in a dual mode, with a dual operating system that can handle both. Scaling and individualizing offer a solution for dual operating systems. It also helps to have the choice of maintaining two separate operating systems and the capabilities that are needed to switch between the two.

Systems offer the rules, routines and tools that help us operate in our specific context. Leadership interaction is how we use systems to support individuals, teams and networks in applying their knowledge and getting work done.

Scaling adds people-centric features to efficiency where people need to deal with increasing volatility, complexity, uncertainty and ambiguity. Talented people are all different. They come with different ambitions, talents and skills. Individualizing leadership adds agile to efficiency in ways that helps every individual unlock their talent and contribute to create value.

Figure 61 frames scaling as a vertical intervention that requires dual systems, and individualizing as a horizontal intervention in how we use dual systems in support of leadership.

FIGURE 61: SCALING AND INDIVIDUALIZING

SCALING SYSTEMS

The challenge for organizations that operate in a hybrid mode is to scale management with an operating system that spans the entire organization. Hybrid modes demand the dual systems' features of traditional, people-centric or dynamic. People-centric and agile can also do traditional.

Control and change. If you are an organization with a stable platform, but need to speed up change to reduce cost, drive immediate profitability and strengthen competitive advantages, you need to mobilize resources and facilitate self-organization by showing trust in their implementation. That helps create a work environment that supports collaboration.

Engagement and enabling. If you're an entrepreneurial organization with highly engaged people, but need to catch fast changes in the environment, be people-centric and capture new technology-related opportunities, you need to delegate power to teams, tap into networks by providing direction and facilitate everyone moving in one direction. That provides for a work environment that nurtures new relationships.

Figure 62 summarizes scaling with an operating system that addresses two levers: moving in one direction and mobilizing resources with a focus on teams, the institution and networks.

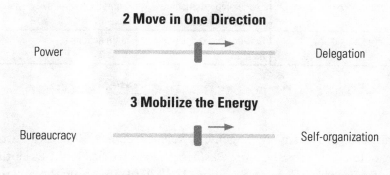

FIGURE 62: SCALING SYSTEMS

How do we move in one direction at scale? (Figure 63) To establish the collective ability to decide on valuable opportunities, organizations need an operating system that offers choice. Such a dual operating system connects people to enhance their knowledge and aligns interests.

Elements	Controls	Systems
Strategy	Strategy as a mental model	A strategy development process for every team
Strategy conversation	Leadership interactions that offers choice	Creative team learning, rigorous strategy reviews
Shared intent	Collective, delegated thinking	Team decisions and alignment

FIGURE 63: THE DUAL SYSTEM TO MOVE IN ONE DIRECTION

How do we mobilize energy at scale? (Figure 64) To establish collective trust in people's ability to deliver in organizations requires practices and tools that help them turn opportunities into value. Such a dual operating system enables self-organization and collaboration at scale.

Elements	Controls	Systems
Implementation	Decentralized performance management	Resource allocation on demand, agile planning and implementation, flexible goals
Performance conversation	Leadership interactions to enhance trust	Rigorous, interactive business reviews
Shared agenda	Self-organized collective action	Team actions

FIGURE 64: THE DUAL SYSTEM TO MOBILIZE THE ENERGY

Stanford University management science expert Robert I Sutton articulated this in a *Harvard Business Review* article, 'Eight Essentials for Scaling Up Without Screwing Up' (2014). In short, he asserted that scaling management is all about the following:

- Spreading a mindset that instils the right beliefs and behaviours
- Scaling may require eliminating traditions, strategies, practices and roles that were once helpful but have outlived their usefulness
- You have two choices: make people believers, and then let them freely localize the rituals, or legislate the behaviour you've identified as being best, and assume that people will become believers and act that way
- Rational arguments for change are insufficient; use positive emotions to channel energy and passion.
- Exposing people to leadership rhetoric is not enough; you should build or find excellence, and use it to guide and inspire more excellence
- Cut cognitive overload but embrace necessary organizational complexity
- Build organizations where people come to feel, 'I own the place, and the place owns me'
- Bad is stronger than good – clear away the things that stand in the way of excellence

INDIVIDUALIZING LEADERSHIP

People who operate in a hybrid mode have a greater need for individual leadership. This is leadership that interacts and supports learning, while at the same time offering clarity and the means to focus attention. This can be achieved through:

- **Offering meaningful work.** Individualizing leaders focus on the why when they discuss work, goals and projects. The idea is that employees come up with their own solutions to problems they're asked to solve.
- **Delegation and feedback.** Individualizing leaders have trust in people and teams, create an environment with degrees of freedom – along with safety – and offer feedback and support at eye level.
- **Learning in network.** Individualizing leaders favour networks over hierarchies, and they enable learning in peer-to-peer contexts.
- **Balancing dual operating systems.** Individualizing leaders operate in ambidextrous ways that stretch between traditional and agile. They adjust their leadership style to what people and context require, without losing consistency.
- **Leading virtually and enabling diversity.** Individualizing leaders interact by analogue means (face-to-face) and digitally. They enable diversity by supporting heterogeneous teams.

It's individuals who search for purpose, connect and build relationships, naturally collaborate and focus attention to learn. But learning is a shared responsibility between individuals and the organization, represented by its leaders. To individualize leadership, we need a dual operating system that combines traditional and agile interactions.

Control and engagement. If you're a successful, well-positioned organization, but want to benefit from digitalization and tap into the knowledge of people, you need empowered people who thrive on self-responsibility through information that raises awareness. They know with clarity, and that makes for a work environment where people find purpose.

Change and enabling. If you're a flexible organization that's always reacting to changes in the environment, but you want to speed up learning, proactively capture opportunities and align dispersed teams, you need to align the means and provide broad direction. This can be achieved through focus of attention, beliefs and boundaries, allowing people to maintain the focus. That makes for a work environment where they can learn.

Figure 65 offers individualizing leadership based on two levers: know with clarity and maintain the focus.

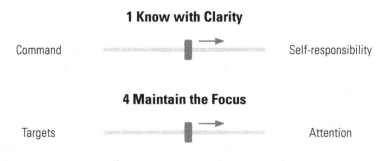

1 Know with Clarity

Command   Self-responsibility

4 Maintain the Focus

Targets   Attention

FIGURE 65: INDIVIDUALIZING LEADERSHIP

How do we individualize to know with clarity? (Figure 66) To establish collective awareness of what matters most, organizations need practices and tools that help people identify opportunities and find purpose. Such a dual operating system enables self-responsible people to act individually.

Elements	Controls	Systems
Information	Feedback information where the work is being done, transparency	Performance measurement as diagnostic information, few metrics, instant feedback
Sense-making	Leadership interactions to create awareness	Sense-making techniques, rigorous meaning creation
Shared understanding	Collective awareness to find purpose	Team insights and analysis

FIGURE 66: THE DUAL SYSTEM TO KNOW WITH CLARITY

How do we individualize how we maintain the focus? (Figure 67) To establish collective attention, organizations need practices and tools that help people stick to identified opportunities. Such a dual operating system establishes focus of attention to learn as individuals.

Elements	Controls	Systems
Beliefs and boundaries	Engagement and governance	Vision, mission, values, performance objectives, risk limits
Contribution and risk dialogues	Leadership interactions to clarify the playing field	Team performance management, rigorous performance reviews
Shared aspirations and norms	Collective engagement through values and broad direction	Team focus of attention

FIGURE 67: THE DUAL SYSTEM TO FOCUS ATTENTION

Individualizing and scaling require ambidextrous capabilities from employees, leaders and the operating system. Stress, conflicts and role ambiguity limit the individual ability for ambidexterity. Diversity in leadership teams is a key factor in following an ambidextrous strategy. Leaders with a diverse background and teams with different experiences are more likely to explore new directions and capabilities while maintaining current operations. However, integrating individualizing and scaling functions in one responsibility tends not to work, and in fact reduces overall ambidexterity. What works is individualizing leadership, and top management ensuring that managerial systems are designed to scale.

People-centric demands interactions with individuals. Interactions are an effective means of control. People-centric interactions are individual and specific to every person. The shift to people-centric demands that leaders be out at the client front, interact with stakeholders and 'interfere' as the means to exercise control. As interactions become more intense and take up a large part of senior executives' time, it makes sense to delegate some of the organizing and planning work to a chief of staff (by a CEO), to an assistant (by senior leaders) or to junior managers (for other leaders). They can give you time to be with your people at the client front. Chiefs of staff can triage data and feed to leaders what they need in order to lead.

Scaling and individualizing are two complementary features of a dual operating system, for organizations wanting to make the shift, operate in a hybrid mode, and enable People-Centric Management. Scaling addresses the systems, to operate in a dynamic environment, and individualizing updates leadership in the context of distributed knowledge. Intervention in any operating system is a transformation, as they alter the behaviours, decisions and actions of people in organizations.

In this chapter, we explored how dynamic makes dual operating systems work by combining traditional and people-centric. We've expanded on scaling and individualising the toolbox to balance efficiency with innovation.

THE DUAL OPERATING SYSTEM

More often than not, your organization operates in a hybrid mode. That's when your operating system requires dual features.

KEY CHAPTER IDEAS

- Your operating system needs to scale and individualize
- Dual practices and tools work with both traditional and people-centric
- Distinct dynamic controls and tools add dual to your operating system

ACTION AGENDA

Find out whether your organization needs a dual operating mode:
- Identify your hybrid mode
- Select the practices and tools that fit your mode

FURTHER READING

Kleiner, A (2008). *The Age of Heretics: A History of the Radical Thinkers Who Reinvented Corporate Management*. San Francisco: Jossey-Bass.

Pfeffer, J (1998). *The Human Equation: Building Profits by Putting People First*. Boston, Harvard Business School Press.

CHAPTER

IT'S A TRANSFOR-MATION

It's time to get hands-on with making the shift to people-centric. Imagine that you and your management team have decided on people-centric, built on a stable foundation, with People-Centric Management at its core. How do you make that shift?

So far, we have answered the 'why' and 'what' questions. Next, we'll focus on the 'how.' The question becomes, 'How people-centric are we?' If the answer leaves something to be desired, the follow-up is, 'How do we get there?' This chapter explains how to make the shift and enable People-Centric Management at scale.

Earlier, we discussed the shift from control to enabling, and from traditional to people-centric, with a focus on what's needed in an agile organization. But the initial mind shift initiates with you as a leader. The shift comes through a high awareness that traditional is no longer sufficient in a dynamic environment. Diagnostic tools can establish that awareness with teams at scale. The insights gained from diagnostic results help you design and decide on what works best for your organization. Then, initial experience, by *doing it,* expedites the learning. There's no shortcut to awareness, focus and trust, which comprise the mindset needed to make the transformation and build the capabilities.

Will the transformation just happen? I've made the point that agile is new for most people and organizations, and that it requires experience to get there. How can we do something without that experience?

Can you rely on a people-centric movement? I have 'borrowed' many of the historical insights of the management writer David Hurst (2018), whom I've gotten to know over the past decade at the Global Drucker Forum in Vienna. On the somewhat pessimistic side, he argues that the Anglo-Saxon mindset is hard to overcome.

"Of course, the Cartesians have an answer: 'It takes a conscious choice.' This ignores the fact that mindset is a multi-layered concept," Hurst said. "A mindset can be an explicit model or a broad world view. As we learn, the process of logic breaks down. Knowledge becomes wisdom. The Cartesian 'I' becomes incapable of standing outside the self. From this point on, a change in mindset demands a change in identity, an existential change in the way of being. Changes at that deep level take compelling experiences, not intellectual choices. This will take a social movement and more."

Standardized processes and routines in organizations are inadequate for innovations. It takes a soft and indirect approach – one that calls for multiple perspectives and cooperation. Only when the dual brain becomes fully engaged can humans set aside self-interest and collaborate with their peers on a common cause. It's when experience meets learning and action.

The optimistic view is that agile meets the criteria of an ecological-adaptive approach. The model fits both brains, the logical and the emergent. And, the only way to get there is by cultivating and learning. In successful agile transformations, agile capabilities develop through design thinking, in an emergent, collective, circular mode that draws on creativity, talent and second-order Cybernetics (the observation of systems). In dynamic capabilities theory[5] this is called 'capability monitoring.'

People-centric is a movement. It will take time. There's no reason to wait for it; it won't *just happen*. It's an opportunity to turn people-centric into your organization's competitive advantage (your rational decision). For some executives, a mindset shift is necessary to make that people-centric shift (your trust in your organization's capabilities and experience). The objective: a sustainable transformation with impact.

A word of caution: transformations still have a low success rate despite an abundance of research and practical experience with how they work. Studies consistently report that three quarters of change programmes flop. Failures are often attributed to poor implementation and misdiagnosis of where the change should start or what changes need to be made. My two brains would conclude that failures are due to the predominant chief executive mindset that dominates these traditional programmes and their evaluation.

People-Centric Management transformation refers to fundamental changes in behaviours, in the decision-making, and in the actions of leaders and employees. It's a transformation where left and right brains interact and combine. We do not use the 'transformation' label lightly.

THREE TRIGGERS

We often hear from executive teams that they 'need to be more people-centric.' Unless you've already made that decision, here are three triggers to help you get going. They ask for a change in the design of leadership and systems:

- **Interferences and unused potential:** when your organization lacks performance
- **Faulty operating mode:** when your leadership and systems are stuck in old modes
- **Change in context:** when your business environment has changed

INTERFERENCES AND UNUSED POTENTIAL

When interferences and unused potential limit performance (Figure 68), it's time to consider the people-centric shift. You notice interferences when your leadership requires lots of time to fix what should be normal. When fluctuation increases, it's time to look at unused potential.

Interferences stem from erroneous systems, faulty leadership or a virus-infected culture. All three require a fix. The fix may need a shift to people-centric. For example, tools in the toolbox that don't fit create undesired behaviours. Or, self-responsibility and detailed performance targets don't fit. The results default to control, which limits motivation and engagement.

Unused potential is a major cost driver. It doesn't make sense to hire the best talent and then limit their engagement. Systems and leadership are a frequent cause of such inefficiencies. For example, control-oriented leadership may drive efficiency, but it limits creativity. As we noted earlier, when people take orders, they will follow these orders but do no more. As a result, organizations miss out on the creative potential and, eventually, the innovation capacity.

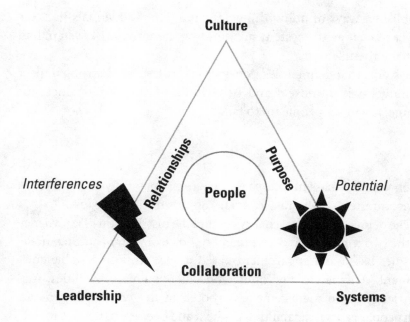

FIGURE 68: INTERFERENCES AND POTENTIAL

What do you fix first: leaders, culture or systems? Imagine that you've decided to make the shift to people-centric. Where do you start your intervention?

Culture? It is an outcome that requires interventions in leadership and systems. Over time, this will result in an effective culture.

Leadership? This is where most fixing starts. But, why would you train leaders to come back in on Monday morning only to find themselves in the same mess?

Here is what works best: first, fix systems, and then train leaders to use them interactively. Over time, this will establish a strong shared culture. Remove systems interference before developing leaders.

In their *Harvard Business Review* article, 'Why Leadership Training Fails, and What to Do About It,' management consultants Michael Beer, Magnus Finnström and Derek Schrader (2016) make the following point: "The problem was that even well-trained and motivated employees could not apply their new knowledge and skills when they returned to their units, which were entrenched in established ways of doing things. In short, the individuals had less power to change the system surrounding them than the system had to shape them."

Systems that define roles, routines and rules have a strong impact on individuals' mindsets and behaviours. If the system does not change, it will set people up to fail.

FAULTY OPERATING MODE

When your business functions in the wrong operating mode, you can expect interferences to take over and opportunities to be lost.

The degree of external challenges and the distribution of knowledge are the two triggers that determine the choice of your operating mode.

Rules-based and engagement-based modes work in a stable environment. A dynamic environment needs dynamic capabilities. And knowledge-based management is rooted in the engagement mode, with people-centric capabilities. Context and operations need to match.

CHANGE IN CONTEXT

When volatility, complexity, uncertainty and ambiguity change, it's time to adjust your operating mode.

For example, fixed performance targets and volatility don't go together. In a fast-changing context, annual goals prevent people from adapting to the change. Remember, targets are agreed upon, so they represent a contract between the employee and the organization. It's unfair to ask an employee to bend a contract and accept a disadvantage in order to follow the change. A system that works well in a stable environment may turn against employees and the organization when the context changes.

How do you know? Over the last 20 years, we have learned that it makes sense to occasionally diagnose your context and the operating system for viruses and unused potential. Such diagnostics offer a neutral outside perspective, with clarity on what requires change and how to initiate that development.

TWO INTERVENTION PATHS

So far, we have explored scaling and individualizing as concurrent interventions to make the shift to people-centric. However, there are two alternative paths that set different priorities for the intervention: disruption or evolution.

Figure 69 outlines both intervention paths. Disruption as an intervention first alters systems to scale agility, and then develops leadership to individualize People-Centric Management. Conversely, evolution first trains leaders on people-centric, and then scales people-centric throughout their organizations.

FIGURE 69: TWO INTERVENTION PATHS

It's a choice with different assumptions. Disruptions assume that behaviours change through altering the rules, routines and tools for people to get work done. And, they assume that once these systems are designed to address a dynamic environment, it's time to train leaders on the use of systems to enable People-Centric Management. On the contrary, evolution assumes that leaders with the right attitude and mindset can engage in People-Centric Management and then make the change of systems for a dynamic context.

Philosopher and organizational behaviour author Charles Handy, in his seminal book, *The Second Curve*, introduced an S-shaped curve as a means to project the future. The S-shape indicates an initial period of investments, when input exceeds the output. As results begin to show and progress emerges, the line moves up. But there is a time, inevitably, when the curve peaks and begins its descent. The good news is that there's always a second curve. Disruptive innovations (Christensen, 2015) create that second curve.

Traditional management (Figure 70) evolved along the first curve over the past 100 years. It was a success story during a period of relative stability. People-Centric Management is the second curve that disrupts the tradition and will continue to evolve. When speed is important, but systems and processes slow you down, you know that disruption has arrived. Management, organization and leadership are at an inflection point between traditional and people-centric.

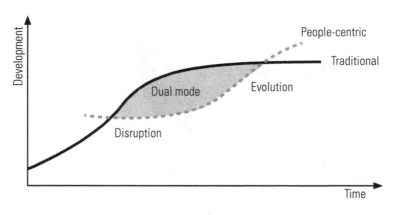

FIGURE 70: A TRANSFORMATION

Dynamic disrupts traditional management, but traditional will continue for a while. In fact, efficiency and reliability attributes will be needed more than ever to delight customers. Neither will go away altogether. The transformation means that both traditional and dynamic will coexist and perform as intended: traditional for exploitation and dynamic (agile) for exploration. This coexistence will require the hybrid mode of operations with a dual operating system.

Over time, evolution replaces disruption. The transformation mode shift will take you from adapting the operating system to training leaders and employees how to be effective in the agile mode. Training and education will do the job. But, as Harvard Business School's Amy Edmondson (2018) demonstrates, organizations need 'fertile soil' in place before 'seeds' of training interventions can grow. And, she notes, people need 'psychological safety' at work for transformations to succeed.

Can you first evolve and then disrupt? Companies around the world spend billions annually on employee training and education (Beer, Finnström and Schrader, 2016). The evidence of success is slim. Why do companies continue what clearly does not work?

First, organizations are viewed as aggregations of individuals. By that logic, people must be selected and trained on the right skills, knowledge and attitudes. The expectation is that this then translates into changed organizational capabilities. But organizations and systems consist of interconnected sub-systems and processes that drive behaviour and performance. If systems don't change, they won't support individual behaviour change. Second, it's hard to confront senior executives with the uncomfortable truth that failure to change or implement isn't rooted in individuals' deficiencies, but in the policies and practices created by top management.

WHO IS RESPONSIBLE?

The people-centric shift, whether it's a disruption or an evolution, is about learning. The question becomes one of who's responsible for making the shift in the system happen.

Learning has three roles: readiness, capabilities and opportunity. Readiness rests with the individual. Learning is an individual accountability. It requires awareness, focus, trust and choice. Capability is a shared responsibility between people and the institution. Leaders need to provide the opportunity. Then, it's up to the individual to capture that opportunity. Opportunity resides with the institution. It is the institution's role to provide the opportunity. As such, institutions and individuals have different roles and accountabilities to make the shift to people-centric.

But, without exception, any decision to pursue an agile transformation lies with top management. It fundamentally alters the DNA of the organization. It assumes self-responsibility, which is an altogether different image of mankind. Decisions are delegated to the client front. Networks of teams organize themselves. And, broad objectives inspire people and maintain their focus. Systems, leadership and culture are at stake.

At the same time, this dramatic change alters the role of leaders. It's their task to establish a work environment where people can unlock their full talent. And, leaders control through interaction – their onsite presence and support for people to get work done.

A people-centric transformation alters the functioning of an entire organization. Team or department-level change projects without the consent to alter systems, leadership and culture are doomed to fail.

HOLISTIC AND COMPLEMENTARY

As we have seen, systems, leadership and culture frame the operating system of an organization. These elements complement each other and depend on each other. Developing People-Centric Management requires a holistic approach that addresses all elements. Quick fixes on one element miss the point. Systems and leadership are constraints on culture (Figure 71).

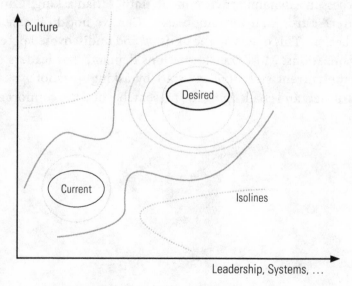

FIGURE 71: CONSTRAINTS ON CULTURE

I often hear, 'We need to change the culture to improve results.' But, culture is an outcome that depends on systems and leadership interventions. You can only intervene by altering your managerial system or updating the skills of leaders. When done in combination, this will improve the overall culture.

The people-centric shift from current capabilities to the desired capabilities requires getting rid of the old and developing the new. Think of it as a mountaineering tour, where you visualize climbing the next peak as you stand on your current peak. You first have to walk down your current mountain to then climb to the desired summit. If your current peak represents your current agile capabilities, and your desired mountain your desired agile capabilities, it becomes clear that the descent requires getting rid of some of the weight of your current capabilities in order to be able to build the desired new capabilities.

In organizational theory, the descent is called 'unlearning.' It is often a necessary step to enable new systems, leadership, behaviours and culture.

But, it's often the case that optimizing the current is insufficient for success in a dynamic environment. Rather than asking, 'Can't we do better?' a true transformation asks, 'Can we not do it *differently* much better?' This opens up the unusual and undiscovered potential in organizations. Most transformations demand that leaders overcome the current system. They start by asking questions, sharing points of view and challenging the present, beyond the comfort zone.

WHERE TO START?

The scale of an organization-wide transformation task is huge. Successful transformations I've seen hardly ever start with a budget or from the top. But, as I have said, people-centric is a capability that permeates an entire organization. As such, department or team efforts to transform to people-centric have little chance of survival.

So, where to start? What are the characteristics of successful transformations? The following is what we have learned from organizations we've accompanied on this journey:

- **It starts with the idea.** Often, the idea comes from an individual who sees the need for a positive approach and seeds the thought. That person can come from anywhere in the organization. Mostly, though, that champion is someone from middle management, positioned close to where the decision is made and connected to people on the ground.

- **It can be anywhere.** Do you need to start at the top, in the middle or with a department? Experience tells us that agile development must range across an organization where people need to collaborate. That can be a department, a geographic unit or an organization as a 'how.' And it must have the right, and the ability, to change systems, leadership and culture.

- **Diagnosis establishes awareness.** Apart from providing the data for the transformation, diagnosis creates awareness of what is and what matters. This is an essential condition for people to contribute with their ideas.

- **Motivation comes from participation.** People-centric capabilities are context- and organization-specific. People-centric is individual to every leader. Hence, engaging leaders and employees in evaluating and developing agile is a must.

- **Design creates prototypes.** People-centric capabilities are specific and in need of tailoring. Copy and paste does not work. People-centric, for most, is untested ground. It requires a decision on mindsets, skill sets and toolsets. That decision is all about design. Prototypes help keep options open and refinement loops going.
- **It's a development, not a project.** People-centric principles require design and development based on an organic and people-centric approach. Traditional project management is built on traditional management concepts, with control and command in mind. It's the best way to kill the idea at square one. Having said that, agile development is focused and disciplined. Progress will be assessed, and feedback helps steer adjustments based on what's been learned.
- **Top management must support it.** The transformation changes management from traditional to people-centric. And, the accountability for managerial systems lies with management. It's a responsibility that cannot be delegated. Top management must establish the umbrella, the frame and the mindset for the transformation.
- **A mentor can help.** Because there is nothing new in this world, external experience can help accelerate the development. Reflection, diversity and interaction with people from different backgrounds stimulate the conversations and energize the development. I believe that most organizations possess the capabilities to make the transformation. Occasional mentoring keeps the development on track.

Keeping these characteristics in mind will help you figure out what the transformation might look like in your organization.

A SYSTEMIC INTERVENTION

Any transformation is an intrusion into a system. That's why it's worth borrowing from the leading systems thinkers.

The environmental scientist Donella Meadows, co-author of a 1972 Club of Rome report, 'The Limits to Growth,' knows a great deal about sustainable transformations. Her manuscript for an unpublished book, *Dancing with Systems* (Meadows, 2001), suggests viewing management and organization as your system:

- **Get the beat.** Before any interference in a system, watch what it does. This keeps you from falling too quickly into your own beliefs, which are subject to natural bias. What does the system do? How did it get there?

- **Listen to the wisdom of the system.** Systems run themselves. Before you intervene to 'make things better,' pay attention to the value it already brings. Don't destroy a system's self-maintenance capacity.

- **Expose your mental model to the open air.** Hold your model up to the scrutiny of peers who challenge assumptions and add their own. Everything everybody knows is only a model. Flexibility to rethink the model is needed in a dynamic setting.

- **Stay humble. Remain a learner.** Trust your intuition more than your rationality. Use both, but be prepared for surprises. When learning, rely on small steps, constant monitoring and willingness to change course as you find out more. Honour, facilitate and protect timely and accurate information.

- **Locate responsibility in the system.** Intrinsic responsibility means that the system is designed to send feedback directly and quickly to the decision-maker. Pay attention to triggering events, the outside influencers.

- **Make feedback policies for feedback systems.** In a dynamic environment, systems need effective control and governance that adapt to the systems state. This means not only feedback loops, but loops that modify and extend loops. These second-order policies design learning into management.
- **Pay attention to what's important, not to what is quantifiable.** The measurement mantra has taken over in organizations, but most of what makes up an organization are the intangibles. Quality, not quantity, is the outstanding characteristic in this world.
- **If something is ugly, say so.** If it's tacky, inappropriate, out of proportion, unsuitable, morally degrading, ecologically impoverishing, or humanly demeaning, don't let it happen. If you don't speak up on what systems are not designed for, they'll continue to exist and infect your system.
- **Go for the good of the whole.** Don't optimize parts of systems while ignoring the whole. Aim to enhance total systems capabilities, such as creativity, stability, diversity, resilience and sustainability. Parts of the system cannot survive without the whole system.
- **Expand time horizons.** Business schedules follow quarterly results, annual budgets and three-year strategies. Systems don't distinguish between short term and long term. Actions sometimes have immediate effects, and they sometimes span decades. You therefore need to watch, short term and long term.
- **Expand thought horizons.** Systems span traditional disciplinary lines. To understand systems, observe them and learn from economists, chemists, psychologists, theologians, philosophers and others. Interdisciplinary conversation beats particular lenses when it comes to solving real-life problems.
- **Expand the boundary of caring.** Life in a world of complex systems requires greater breadth of caring. There are moral reasons to do that. Systems thinking provides the practical reasons to back up the moral ones. They are not separate. People know the interconnections.
- **Celebrate complexity.** Fact is that the world is non-linear, turbulent, chaotic, and poses its share of wicked problems. It's dynamic.

It self-organizes and evolves. It creates diversity, not uniformity. That's what makes the world interesting and what makes it work. Straight lines and simple structures are human constructs. Nature designs fractals, with detail in every scale.

- **Hold fast to the goal of goodness.** Examples of bad behaviour and action are held up, amplified and affirmed by culture. The far more numerous examples of human goodness are barely noticed. They're not news. We know what to do about eroding goals. Don't weigh the bad more than the good. Keep standards absolute.

As an experienced leader, you'll certainly note how Meadows' guidelines have been woven into the four principles, the people-centric shift and transformation. People-Centric Management foremost is an operating system transformation.

WHERE TO INTERVENE?

We continue with Meadows, to explore what she called 'Leverage Points: Places to Intervene in Systems.' Leverage points are where a small shift in one thing can produce big changes in everything. Meadows offers distinct places to intervene in systems, as summarized here, in eight levers arrayed in order of increasing effectiveness:

1. **Constants, parameters, numbers, resources** (subsidies, taxes, standards). It's like rearranging deckchairs on the Titanic. A lot of attention goes into these factors, but there's not a lot of leverage in them.
2. **Regulating negative feedback loops.** It's about buffers and stabilizing stocks. A buffer is like money in the bank rather than living off the flow of change through your pocket. These loops have a self-correcting, stabilizing effect. But changing them is still low on the effectiveness scale.
3. **Driving positive feedback loops.** These loops are self-reinforcing. They are the sources of the growth and the ultimate collapse of a system. A system with positive feedback loops will eventually destroys itself. However, they're quite rare. Look for interest rates, infection rates and more. Carefully observe them.
4. **Information flows.** Who does and does not have access to information? Missing feedback is one of the most common causes of systems malfunction. It's a leverage point that counteracts the tendency of humans to avoid accountability for decisions.
5. **The rules of the system.** The rules – incentives, punishments, constraints – define the scope, boundaries and degrees of freedom of a system. Changing rules is powerful. Power over rules is *really* powerful.

6. **The distribution of power over the rules of the system.** It's the power to add, change, evolve or self-organize system structure. Self-organization means changing any aspect of a system lower on this list. But, self-organization is the strongest form of resilience in a system. The intervention point is obvious, but changing it means losing control.

7. **The goals of the system.** It's the push for control, to bring more and more under central planning. Exchanging people in a system is a low-effectiveness lever. But, there's an exception: changing a single player at the top may give power to change the system's goal.

8. **The mindset or paradigm.** It's the shared idea, the assumptions, the deepest beliefs about how things work. Paradigms are the sources of systems out of which their goals, power structure, rules and culture arise. Paradigms can be changed by modelling systems, which takes you outside the system and forces you to see the whole. It's hard, but not impossible.

The systems view of levers helps us respect that changes in systems matter. The people-centric shift and the transformation are interferences in the system of organization and management. That's why we have given thought to how to make the people-centric shift a successful transformation. It combines systems thinking and social technologies into a three-step process. I recommend that any leader who talks about transformation should first read about systems. It's a rewarding investment of time.

To summarize, with the words of management consultants Gary Hamel and Michele Zanini (2016), a transformation such as eliminating bureaucracy for people-centric "is emergent, collaborative, iterative, and inescapable – one that rolls up rather than rolls out."

THREE
STEPS

The people-centric shift is a transformation where no one has the answers on the specific tools and practices that make up an agile organization, dynamic systems and People-Centric Management. It's a capability that requires individual design to fit it to the specific needs of the organization and its stakeholders. As such, the people-centric shift is a transformation that follows design thinking in three steps: Collectively raise awareness, act on insights and learn fast.

1. **Raise awareness.** Diagnose current capabilities, create awareness
2. **Act on insights.** Identify the desired capability insights for decisions
3. **Learn fast.** Enable People-Centric Management through agile capabilities and dynamic systems

If you look at steps as part of a stairway, you can walk up and down these stairs. If you look at steps as a sequence of stages or things, you can go forward but also backwards. You can take a step back. The three-step transformation works like that. It's not a prescription for a start, then one step, then two, then three, and finished. They represent three mandatory parts that logically follow each other. But, more often than not, one goes back to 'step one' for a fresh look. The steps are circular in how they're applied.

The three-step shift combines individual, team and organizational perspectives into a coherent approach. It establishes an institutional framework for a reflective opening of perspectives through authentic dissent as a tool to learn about people-centric. The exchange and dissent on observations is what creates new insights and knowledge. Interaction and discourse are based on a common language that establishes a shared language.

Figure 72 looks at capabilities that can be observed, modelled and transformed. In a systems view, monitoring and 'dynamization' can be treated as two separate functions. (Luhmann, 1995). Cybernetics calls this second-order observing systems (Von Foerster, 1984). The way we do things becomes a subject of reflection, and opened up to alternatives. Through observation, capabilities become revisable.

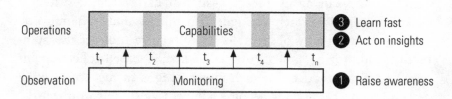

FIGURE 72: CAPABILITY MONITORING

STEP 1: RAISE AWARENESS

Are current capabilities in support of people-centric? Step 1 diagnoses current operations and the context to understand what needs to become people-centric.

Monitoring is the discipline to observe and alter capabilities. By observing (scanning) capabilities, potential faults and malfunctions can be spotted at an early stage. By becoming aware of critical signals, potential design requirements can be identified. With this, leaders can decide whether or not to address the issues. As such, monitoring initiates changes of capabilities.

Distance, new perspectives, critique and multi-voice input are integral parts of the monitoring. Taking a step back, observing and challenging the use of capabilities compensates for the risks of getting locked in. And so, organizations need to review their tools, routines and behaviours in view of their specific context.

Monitoring is risk management. The use of managerial tools and processes is selective. For every context, leaders select the specific systems that support them in managing their organization in that specific context. When the context changes, the toolbox also needs to change.[7] Diagnosing systems, leadership and culture prevents organizations from misapplying tools, ignoring critical events or getting threatened by changes in their operating context.

Taking a distant stance, observation and critique of design and capabilities helps compensate for risks such as thoughtless reproduction of organizational designs and capabilities through path dependency, structural inertia and lock-in. Early warning systems, including monitoring and reflection,[9] can help reduce these risks.[10] This first step, raising awareness, is such an early warning system.

People-centric principles, agile capabilities and dynamic systems are not directly observable. They require indirect measurement.[11] Monitoring as institutionalized, rules-based reflection[12] is a non-routine practice.[13] If such monitoring is to succeed, it must be kept open; it must not become subject to closing routinization. Only then is it possible to detect extraordinary signals that call the validity of current design and capabilities into question.

Monitoring must include the internal and external environment. While internal factors can be identified, external factors are wide open and largely without boundaries. Crises are regularly preceded by weak signals. The interpretation of weak signals requires skills (Ansoff, 1980).

Design scanning and observation should follow systematic methods for generating, modifying and improving capabilities. The monitoring routines themselves need to be updated repeatedly to prevent traps and path-effects. Professional agile insights diagnostics ensure effective monitoring, with continuous investments in the tool to prevent these traps.

It is important to encourage all units, sub-units and members of an organization to actively participate in capability monitoring. Providing a supportive context and social climate is therefore a salient task for effective monitoring. Leadership briefings establish the context and set the rules for a non-political approach to design monitoring.

Capability monitoring is too costly to own and perform in-house for most organizations. Rather, it makes sense to use an outside supplier with expertise, experience and investment in professional diagnostics.

STEP 2: ACT ON INSIGHTS

What is needed for a people-centric design? In Chapters 3-10, we provided the logic to identify, select and align capabilities. Now, Step 2 is about how to design agile capabilities and dynamic systems and intervene with the insights from the diagnostic.

As mentioned, the use of capabilities and design is selective. The decision on a specific design excludes other alternatives. For People-Centric Management, design is about the selection of managerial tools, routines and rules that make organizations agile. Design requires reflection and interactions. It is not free of politics. The setting for these conversations determines much of the design quality.

As we know all too well, organizations are not free of politics.[14] There is ample bargaining over goals, interest and values. The three-step shift needs to combine design thinking with facilitation techniques into an intervention that helps bridge diverging views on how to manage and organize.

In our data-driven times, analysis has become the predominant way we look at the world. We're rationally compelled by the logic of the idea and assume that feelings will naturally follow. Logic and data combine to produce a cognitive 'sense of proof.' The academic and author Roger L Martin said that in today's world, logic plus data provides proof, which generates emotional comfort, which leads to directly to commitment (Martin, 2017). "[T]he tricky thing about new ideas is that there is no data yet to analyse – otherwise the idea wouldn't be new," Martin wrote. "The absence of data undermines our modern commitment equation. For the new idea, the equation is likely to be: logic without data produces speculation, which results in emotional discomfort. And a consequence: an over commitment to exploitation over exploration."

Earlier, I introduced systems theory, citing the work of Donella Meadows. Another foundation of systems thinking came from the social scientist Niklas Luhmann. His focus is on systems-based sociology. He claims that sociology – and with it, systems-based sociology – "ist die Wissenschaft des zweiten Blicks" (is the science of the second opinion). But nobody depends on a second opinion. A second opinion is a luxury. Systems-based external descriptions are an important element of systems theory and practical in use. The challenge is that communication on alternatives often interferes with the self-creation and development tendency (autopoiesis) of systems. Rash pronouncements like, 'It's time to do things – enough conversation,' prevent people from exploring good alternatives.

Design thinking is the methodology that helps us find new ways of exploring the future and how we do things. It combines both the logic and the emotions. Commitment comes from the balance of the two.

Design thinking is about reflection[15] and interaction. Reflection is a systems perspective that limits resistance to change that is inherent in any individual's perspective. Guided interactions among participants deal with politics in organizations. They serve as a framework for action.

People-centric is new information and new knowledge for most leaders, employees and organizations. Design initiates the immediate learning.[16] Effective learning of new knowledge and behaviours requires a supportive environment. Workshops where all participants are involved in the diagnostics create such an environment.

Building on agile methodologies, design thinking is a collaborative, customer-centric and iterative approach. For example, the team workshop is a setting where all participants apply their knowledge and insights to come up with alternatives for the challenges the diagnosis might reveal. The goal is to come up with a list of five to seven things the team has decided to work on. The team workshop combines individual, team and organizational perspectives.[17] It establishes the setting for interactions among leaders and employees that neutralize the inevitable effects of bias, power and traps. Does any of this add value to our customers?

Authentic dissent[18] through multiple perspectives is an important function of capability monitoring. This is why it's advisable to retain an outside partner with expert knowledge to balance valuable diverging views on the interpretation of diagnostic results. Creating a 'naysayer culture' is another important element of such workshops. An effective team workshop follows a strict set of rules[19] for these conversations.

STEP 3: LEARN FAST

How do we enable People-Centric Management? With clarity on the design, Step 3 is about making people-centric a competitive advantage for operations in a dynamic environment. It follows the principles of inner game learning.

Monitoring assumes that design is reversible and not frozen in place. While deeply embedded in organizational practices and rooted in the past, managerial design and capabilities can be changed through interventions.[20]

The people-centric shift guides specific capability development projects in line with the decision on what needs to be changed. With this, the idea of permanent change is replaced by the notion of combined learning and doing (Schreyögg and Noss, 2000). It's an iterative process.

People-centric principles stress that the way executives envisage the outcome and rally available resources defines a firm's destination (Eisenhardt and Martin, 2000; Penrose, 1959). Moreover, learning processes have an integrative influence that leads to a creative use of resources in a dynamic environment (Easterby-Smith and Prieto, 2008). And so, development and learning processes are central to the application of people-centric and agile capabilities (Zahra et al., 2006). The ecological and evolutionary theories of the firm posit that strong inertial forces severely constrain the organization's capacity to adapt to changes in the environment (Nelson and Winter, 1982).

Many studies have noted that the capacity for learning and adaptation varies across organizations, and these differences appear to be caused by deeply rooted management actions, policies and decisions (Bloom and van Reenen, 2007).

Visual thinking heavily impacts the cognitive effectiveness of learning in a business context (Gavrilova et al., 2013). Over the last two decades, visual thinking has become an integral part of knowledge sharing, collaborative learning, problem solving and developing competencies. Sketching, mapping, visual protocolling and graphical concepts have become part of everyday managerial practices. Today, visualization supports a variety of mental processes in learning, such as perception, memorization and development (Scocco, 2008).

Concept maps provide structures and mental models that support the learning (Sowa, 1984). Strategy maps and scorecards have been in use in businesses for many years, combining performance measurement techniques and visual presentations.

In stable markets, the refinement of people-centric principles, agile capabilities and dynamic systems helps to capture and defend competitive advantages. In highly dynamic markets, incremental change is not sufficient. Often, radical transformation is required.

THINGS TO REMEMBER

Experienced leaders know that transforming management and organization to people-centric is not easy. Here are some of the things that increase the odds of success:

- **Authorization.** A people-centric transformation fundamentally alters the design of organization and management. Don't hire agile coaches to work with specific teams, and start changing things around, without the consent and support of top management. People-centric requires work on the system. And that is, by definition, top management's responsibility.
- **Diagnosis.** Why would you want to guess if you can know? Transformations always start with clarity on where to start. With that starting point, your transformation can be specific, and address those interferences that keep you from exploiting the potential, rather than a broad range of change initiatives that have little to do with the problem to be solved.
- **Design.** Any people-centric transformation requires changes in rules, routines and tools. New things can only be adopted through the transformation's unique design and self-driven development. Don't copy from consultants or other organizations. Resistance and lack of fit will increase interferences – and lead to further resistance – rather than support the transformation.
- **Priority.** A transformation always happens on current operations; it's effectively 'open-heart surgery.' It is important to be clear that serving clients has top priority. One should pace transformation efforts in ways that do not disturb or interrupt ongoing client operations. Also, it is good practice to do a bit of 'spring cleaning' on systems and routines before creating new ones.

DO WHAT YOU SAY YOU WILL DO

I was invited by the cosmetics division of a large consumer products company to give a talk about people-centric. The assignment was to introduce the concept to its manufacturing leaders. The company was up against competition that was much nimbler and faster in adapting to changing consumer demands. In preparation for the briefing, I gathered media coverage of the company as a whole. There were lots of articles about the new group CEO, anticipating efficiency goals and another change programme. Rumour had it that the company would launch the latest in a string of restructuring efforts, with a reduction in workforce.

During my remarks, I asked about the opposing messages of efficiency (exploitation) and agile. The response was that agile was what they needed, and I accepted the task. This was a mistake. I failed miserably in trying to explain people-centric and agile to manufacturing leaders who only had efficiency gains in mind. I learned my lesson the hard way.

In any people-centric transformation, the message needs to fit the action on the ground. Failure to do that will inevitably result in a failed transformation. People's senses are tuned to listen to the differences between what is said and what is done.

This chapter focused on how people-centric we are and what we can do. We explored the shift to people-centric as a transformation that scales, and an individualizing intervention that you can either make as a disruption or an evolution. In any case, the shift follows the three design thinking steps: create awareness, act on insights and learn fast.

IT'S A TRANSFORMATION

The three-step people-centric transformation approach applies systems theory and its practice enacts People-Centric Management.

KEY CHAPTER IDEAS

- Three triggers help you evaluate the need for change
- It requires both disruption and evolution
- It's a transformation in three steps: awareness, insights, learning

ACTION AGENDA

If you develop people-centric, do it the agile way:
- Decode: apply irregular systemic feedback
- Design: align levers, and create tools and practices
- Develop: enable people to apply their talent to succeed

FURTHER READING

Martin, RL (2017). Use Design Thinking to Build Commitment to a New Idea. *Harvard Business Review*, 3. January.

Kotter, JP (1995). Leading Change: Why Transformation Efforts Fail. *Harvard Business Review*, March-April, 59-67.

Hurst, DK (2014). *The New Ecology of Leadership: Business Mastery in a Chaotic World.* New York: Columbia University Press.

Michel, L (2017). *Management Design: Managing People and Organizations in Turbulent Times* (Second ed.). London: LID Publishing.

Beer, M; Eisenstat, RA; and Spector, B (1990). Why Change Programs Don't Produce Change. *Harvard Business Review,* November-December.

CHAPTER **12**

WITH
PEOPLE
IN MIND

Imagine that you and your team have successfully made the shift to people-centric. There is one more thing to think about: how do you expect your managers to succeed in today's dynamic context and make people-centric their way to lead?

This chapter brings it all together. It offers four levers that combine people-centric principles and the means for every leader to enable people-centric in your organization. Put people first on your list of priorities. Five activities transform your organization and management, allowing leaders to harness the talent of their people and bring out the greatness of others. It's about good management and leadership everywhere.

WORK *IN* THE SYSTEM

Business is about identifying, selecting and transforming opportunities into value. With the people in mind, managers can now use the four principles as their means to deliver value with their teams in a dynamic environment. People-centric managers apply the following principles with their teams (Figure 73):

1. **Know with Clarity:** raise awareness. Help people find purpose. They know that motivation stems from self-responsibility. Purpose replaces incentives. All leaders need to do for people is help them make sense of what truly matters. That's the best way to identify opportunities and deal with the complexity in your business.

2. **Move in One Direction:** enable choice. Relate with people to enhance knowledge. People-centric leaders delegate decisions and relate with people to enhance their skills and knowledge. Choice and direction are their means to bundle the energy, help them select the right opportunities and move in one direction as their way to deal with ambiguity.

3. **Mobilize the Energy:** build trust. Facilitate collaboration. People-centric leaders facilitate self-organization based on trust as the means to deal with uncertainty. They mobilize resources in ways that enable collaboration across organizational boundaries, which turns opportunities into value.

4. **Maintain the Focus:** focus attention. Enable learning. People-centric leaders use beliefs and boundaries to keep attention centred on what truly matters. They know that focus enables learning as the means to unlock creativity, and to stick with chosen opportunities, despite the temptations of higher volatility.

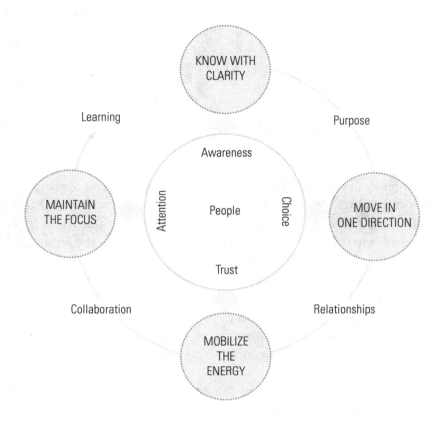

FIGURE 73: PEOPLE-CENTRIC MANAGEMENT

Applying People-Centric Management is work *in* the system. You should expect all your managers to follow these four principles and develop their enabling approach to management, which caters to the people as individuals.

SET YOUR PRIORITIES

The Performance Triangle helps you establish people-centric, agile, client-focused and dynamic capabilities at scale, with the right priorities in mind (Figure 74). The hierarchy becomes: people first (they are in the centre); agile organization second (the operating environment); clients third (work environment: your job to be done); and dynamic operations fourth (your responsibility as a manager).

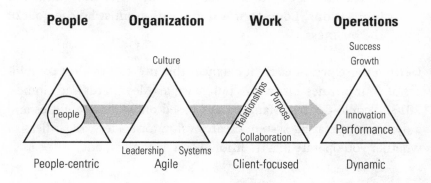

FIGURE 74: MANAGEMENT PRIORITIES

People-centric managers establish an environment along four priorities, so keep this in mind while you work *on* the system:

1. **People are the centre of your attention.** People-centric demands an individual environment where people can unlock their talent and perform at their peak. It's people who deliver value to clients. They should be able to experience flow, the state where challenges and capabilities meet to create a positive experience. That's the ultimate goal of People-Centric Management. As a leader, it is your task (and your obligation) to create that kind of work environment.

2. **Your organization sets the context.** Agile capabilities enable People-Centric Management. Systems, leadership and culture establish the operating environment for people to apply their talent and perform. Hence, it is important to be clear about the potential and interferences in your own organization.

3. **It's people who care about clients.** People-centric principles enable you as a leader to demand self-responsibility, delegate work, enable self-organization and lead with broad directives. This means that the people in your organization can take charge and take care of clients. Client-focus is all about your people making sure that valuable clients are satisfied, come back and want more.

4. **Success is what attracts owners.** They look for growth and return on their investment. Growth comes from clients who come back. Returns come from efficiency gains and innovations. Long-term value creation must be the goal of the business.

Getting these priorities right balances the interests of all stakeholders of your business. It creates public value (Meynhardt and Gomez, 2013). People-Centric Management based on agile capabilities and a dynamic operating system creates value for society, regardless of whether you operate in a traditional or a dynamic mode.

WORK *ON* THE SYSTEM

People-Centric Management balances effectiveness and innovation in five activities (Figure 75): understand context, identify principles, design levers, apply people-centric and lead people with their greatness in mind.

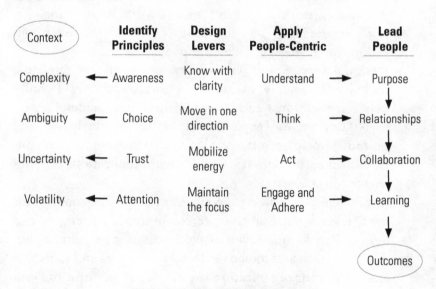

FIGURE 75: LEADING PEOPLE

Every part requires your work *on* the system:

- **Understand context.** With increasing complexity, ambiguity, uncertainty and volatility, agile capabilities help your organization quickly adapt to the new environment. They resolve the tensions between the challenges of the new context and the need for clarity, direction, energy and focus. Part 1 is about raising awareness in your team that the context has changed, which launches the quest for people-centric principles.

- **Identify principles.** People are best equipped to resolve the tensions the new context poses. They apply four inner-game principles – awareness, choice, trust and attention – to address the challenges of the outer game. Part 2 is your choice for People-Centric Management in line with these principles. Applying the inner game is a mindset question that has implications on the design of the four people-centric levers.

- **Design levers.** Know with clarity, move in one direction, mobilize the energy, maintain the focus, and offer a choice between traditional and People-Centric Management. Part 3 is your decision for People-Centric Management with a choice on four principles: self-organization, delegation, self-responsibility and attention. It's a choice with implications for your leadership skill set.

- **Apply agile.** Following People-Centric Management calls for five managerial tasks: understand, think, act, engage and adhere. Part 4 requires you to make a decision on your Leadership Scorecard and toolbox with rules, routines and tools that leaders in your organization use at scale to perform the four tasks. You will have to think about the right design of your systems, leadership and culture.

- **Lead people.** With the right design of your toolbox, your leaders establish purpose as the source of motivation, connect people to nurture relationships, facilitate collaboration as a means to coordinate work, and expedite learning as the means to perform, innovation and grow.

We have explored in depth what every part of the foundation and the shift means for the design of your Leadership Toolbox.

Use People-Centric Management to get your team to design the dynamic toolbox that fits the people-centric approach, and apply the principles to help you deal with a dynamic environment and deliver superior business outcomes. Here is what you can rely on:

- The **inner game** as the individual guide to reconcile tensions
- The **performance triangle** with its agile elements
- The **means of work** for enhanced customer focus
- The **levers** for the shift from traditional to people-centric
- The **dynamic toolbox** to bridge people, organization and context
- The **dual operating system** that enables scaling and individualizing
- The **transformation** that fundamentally alters behaviours and actions
- The **insights and steps** for you to personally shift to people-centric
- The **management cycle** that will establish greatness with your team

Now, it's up to you to make the shift and manage the people-centric way.

PEOPLE ARE
THE ENDS

People-centric, agile and dynamic capabilities enable People-Centric Management. I have never said that this is easy. There are no three simple steps, easy recipes, best practices or readily available consultancy advice. I continue to emphasize that developing these capabilities needs to follow people-centric principles. Design thinking guides the three steps. First, be aware of where your organization starts from. Second, design the capabilities based on diagnostic insights. Third, develop People-Centric Management by engaging all your experts and leaders in the process.

There is no one else who can close the loop any better. Author Charles Handy put it this way: "People are human beings – not human capital. They are the ends of leadership."

WITH PEOPLE IN MIND

Applying People-Centric Management is the key to greatness in a dynamic context. Making the shift to people-centric is what it takes to get there.

KEY CHAPTER IDEAS

Work *on* the system. Design systems with people in mind, in five parts:

1. Understand context: volatility, uncertainty, complexity and ambiguity
2. Identify principles: awareness, choice, trust and attention
3. Design four levers: know with clarity, move in one direction, mobilize energy and maintain the focus
4. Apply people-centric: understand, think, act, engage and adhere
5. Lead with people in mind: purpose, relationships, collaboration and learning

ACTION AGENDA

Work *in* the system. Lead the people-centric way:

- Raise awareness: help people find purpose
- Enable choice: relate with people to enhance knowledge
- Build trust: facilitate collaboration
- Focus attention: enable learning

FURTHER READING

Handy, C (2019). *21 Letters on Life and its Challenges.* London: Hutchinson.

Hamel, G (2007). *The Future of Management.* Boston: Harvard Business School Press.

Michel, L (2020). *Agile by Choice: How You Can Make the Shift to Establish Leadership Everywhere.* London: LID Publishing.

Nayar, V (2010). *Employees First, Customers Second.* Boston: Harvard Business School Press.

PEOPLE-CENTRIC DIAGNOSTIC

The shift to people-centric with agile capabilities is a transformation. It fundamentally alters behaviours, decision-making, and the actions of leaders and employees. Success is not guaranteed. To raise the odds of coming out on top, this book has outlined the three steps – decode, design and develop – organizations can follow to successfully make the shift to people-centric. The People-Centric Diagnostic initiates the process.

This process offers 20 questions, and various visual thinking aids, for you and your team to establish the base from where to start, debate priorities, and decide on the choices for your transformation. The diagnostic is a structured way to gather input and knowledge for a hard look at your organization. Clarity on the starting point dramatically increases success rates. The design debate sets the priorities among competing challenges. And, the development decisions help you select the right path for the transformation.

The People-Centric Diagnostic answers two questions:

1. How people-centric is your organization?
2. What can you do to develop People-Centric Management?

The Performance Triangle with the agile capabilities, the Fitness Index and the Agile Maturity Level indicate how people-centric your organization is. These visuals help you spot the interferences and potential in your organization. The Operating Mode helps you identify your desired capabilities, and the Canvas supports the workshop with your team on your diagnostic results.

Here's how to get started: Answer the questions (Parts 1 and 2) below by circling your diagnostic scores (Figures 76 and 77).

	Strongly disagree		Disagree		Neutral		Agree		Strongly agree

Thinking about your organization's operating environment, answer the questions below:

1 We deliver on what we promise to our clients with an attractive strategy and the right capabilities.	0	13	25	37	50	63	75	88	100
2 Leaders and employees share the same understanding about how work is performed.	0	13	25	37	50	63	75	88	100
3 Leaders conduct productive conversations with employees regarding expectations and performance.	0	13	25	37	50	63	75	88	100

Thinking about your department's performance, answer the questions below:

4 Our management policies (e.g. decision-making rights, governance, performance and risk management) guide our decisions, actions and behaviours.	0	13	25	37	50	63	75	88	100
5 Our management processes (e.g. performance measurements and feedback, objectives agreements, business reviews) help us work effectively and efficiently.	0	13	25	37	50	63	75	88	100
6 Our management tools (e.g. performance indicators and targets, visions, values, strategies, risk limits, performance targets) help us set the right priorities and focus work on what matters most.	0	13	25	37	50	63	75	88	100

Thinking about your team dynamic, answer the questions below:

7 We can freely collaborate and exchange information across organizational boundaries for synergies and leverage.	0	13	25	37	50	63	75	88	100
8 We can rely on relevant relationships to support our work.	0	13	25	37	50	63	75	88	100
9 We are able to find purpose in what we do, establish a clear identity, and fully commit to our work.	0	13	25	37	50	63	75	88	100

In relation to how your organization competes and evolves, answer the questions below:

10 Our organization is renowned for innovation. We turn ideas into reality and add value to our clients' projects.	0	13	25	37	50	63	75	88	100
11 Our organization captures relevant opportunities and grows steadily.	0	13	25	37	50	63	75	88	100

Thinking about your own work ethic, answer the following questions:

12 I have access to relevant information and ask for feedback to gain clarity on important things.	0	13	25	37	50	63	75	88	100
13 I am able to focus and maintain my attention on important things without interferences.	0	13	25	37	50	63	75	88	100
14 I have the trust of my team and can mobilize the resources to get things done.	0	13	25	37	50	63	75	88	100
15 I have sufficient choice on what I need to do and how I perform those tasks.	0	13	25	37	50	63	75	88	100
16 At work, I can unfold my full potential, for example, freely use and apply all my knowledge, capabilities, and creativity.	0	13	25	37	50	63	75	88	100

FIGURE 76: QUESTIONS (PART 1) – AGILE CAPABILITIES

	Strongly disagree	Disagree	Neutral		Agree		Strongly agree		

Thinking about how your organization helps people to know with clarity, use the scale to answer these questions: Which statement best fits your situation?

17 Leaders keep information to themselves, tell people what to do, and check on their work	0	13	25	37	50	63	75	88	100	Self-responsible employees find purpose in what they are doing and get work done

Thinking about how your company moves in one direction, use the scale below to answer these questions: Which statement best fits your situation?

18 Leaders have the power and insights to make decisions. They determine work, set goals, and communicate direction	0	13	25	37	50	63	75	88	100	Knowledge is widely distributed with employees that make decisions at the client front and act on them

Thinking about how your organization mobilizes energy, use the scale below to answer these questions: Which statement best fits your situation?

19 Leaders engage in comprehensive budgeting and allocate resources	0	13	25	37	50	63	75	88	100	Self-organization is principles by which we allocate resources on demand and collaborate

Thinking about how your organizations maintains the focus, use the scale below to answer these questions: Which statement best fits your situation?

20 Leaders use a comprehensive set of metrics and detailed performance targets to implement strategy	0	13	25	37	50	63	75	88	100	Our leaders mentor employees on how to best focus attention with a broad set of directional goals

FIGURE 77: QUESTIONS (PART 2) – PEOPLE-CENTRIC POTENTIAL

With the assessment of your agile capabilities and your people-centric potential, transfer the scores into the Performance Triangle (Figure 78) and Dynamic Capabilities (Figure 79).

Now, use colour highlighters to mark your scores as follows:

- Green: high scores (80-100) = high agile capabilities
- Yellow: medium scores (69-79) = medium agile capabilities
- Red: low scores (0-69) = low agile capabilities

Then, label every element with the attribute (following underlined element labels) that best fits your assessment. With your assessment, the Performance Triangle and Dynamic Capabilities become meaningful.

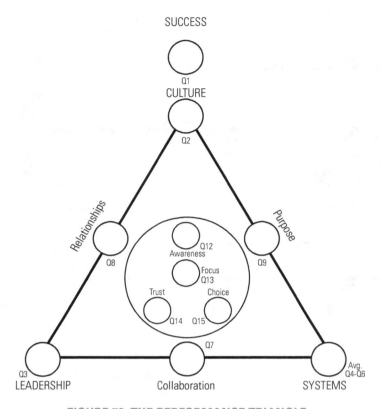

FIGURE 78: THE PERFORMANCE TRIANGLE

The Performance Triangle highlights the agile weaknesses (red scores, missing agile capabilities) and strengths (green scores, existing agile capabilities) in your organization.

Here are the labels for the Performance Triangle:

SUCCESS

- **Sustainable.** A high score means the organization has well-developed capabilities in place that enable superior outcomes
- **Mediocre.** A medium score means the organization has limited capabilities in place, which may prevent superior outcomes
- **Missing.** A low score means the organization has no, or false, capabilities in place, which most likely prevents acceptable outcomes

---

CULTURE

- **Sustainable.** A high score means the team has a shared mindset and agenda
- **Mediocre.** A medium score means the team has a limited shared mindset and agenda
- **Missing.** A low score means the team has no shared mindset or agenda

LEADERSHIP

- **Interactive.** A high score means productive conversations on direction, performance, beliefs and boundaries
- **Busy.** A medium score means limited conversations on direction, performance, beliefs and boundaries
- **Missing or flawed.** A low score means no, or false, conversations on direction, performance, beliefs and boundaries

SYSTEMS

- **Diagnostic.** A high score means reliable systems that are intended to enable collaboration and purpose
- **Bureaucratic.** A medium score means limited systems, which creates friction rather than enabling collaboration and purpose
- **Missing or broken.** A low score means erroneous systems, which prevents collaboration and purpose

PURPOSE

- **Meaningful.** A high score means that people find purpose, are excited, and are energized to contribute
- **Formalized.** A medium score means that people find it hard to see purpose in what they do
- **Missing or distorted.** A low score means that people are demotivated and don't find purpose in what they do

COLLABORATION

- **Intensive.** A high score means that collaboration across boundaries and sharing of knowledge takes place
- **Formalized.** With a medium score, collaboration and sharing of knowledge are controlled by leaders, which is a bottleneck
- **Missing or disrupted.** Low scores mean that silos prevent collaboration and the exchange of information

RELATIONSHIPS

- **Intensive.** A high score indicates strong internal and external relationships that enable people to connect and share their knowledge
- **Formalized.** A medium score indicates limited internal and external relationships, with disconnects and limited sharing of their knowledge
- **Missing or disrupted.** A low score indicates blocked internal and external relationships with no knowledge sharing

AWARENESS

- **Alert.** A high score means high awareness through neutral observation and non-judgmental feedback
- **Obstructed.** A medium score means blurred signals, lots of 'noise' and limited or faulty feedback
- **Blocked or false.** A low score means that signals are on mute, and limited or faulty feedback leads to faulty behaviours and disengagement

FOCUS

- **Bundled.** A high score indicates self-initiated learning and concentration on important things. However, a narrow focus might lead to missed opportunities
- **Blurred.** A medium score means limited learning takes place and people are distracted. This often results in narrow goal orientation rather than focus
- **Distracted or wrong.** A low score means there is distraction and focus on the wrong things. Both lead to underperformance. The most frequent cause is faulty goal orientation rather than lack of focus

TRUST

- **High.** A high score indicates high trust and confidence in personal capabilities. People are responsible for what they are doing
- **Formalized.** A medium score means limited trust and confidence in capabilities. Often, control dominates self-determination
- **Missing or interfered with.** A low score means mistrust in a control-dominated environment

CHOICE

- **High.** A high score means self-determined work with high degrees of freedom and space for creativity
- **Formalized.** A medium score means limited choice and work that is determined by others, with a narrow space for creativity
- **Missing or interfered with.** A low score means no choice on how to get things done. Others determine what is important, without room for creativity

Now, enter your scores in Figure 79, highlight them, and add the label that best fits your assessment.

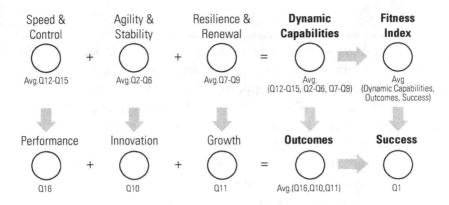

FIGURE 79: DYNAMIC CAPABILITIES

Dynamic capabilities highlight how your organization deliver outcomes.

If you see a lot of green, this means superior capabilities. You're on the best track to unlocking the potential of your people. They demonstrate entrepreneurial behaviours, intense collaboration and a high client focus. Your task is to keep it at that level.

If you see a lot of yellow, this means mediocrity. It's time to break out of the middle ground. Check your organization for how it perfects the art of decision-making, intensifies people interactions and closes the knowing-doing gap. Ensure that you don't miss an opportunity.

If you see a lot of red, this means missing capabilities, and immediate attention is required. Continue the work on your dynamic capabilities.

Here are the labels:

SPEED AND CONTROL

- **High, well-balanced.** A high score means people have the means to perform at their peak
- **Medium, struggling.** A medium score means inferences prevent people from using their full potential. Performance likely suffers
- **Low, unbalanced.** A low score means people don't use their potential. They are bored, stressed or work in an infected environment

AGILITY & STABILITY

- **High, well-balanced.** A high score means the organization has well-developed agile capabilities. The challenge is to keep it up
- **Medium, limited.** A medium score means the organization has room to improve agility. The task is to work on culture, leadership and systems
- **Low, unbalanced.** The organization lacks the capabilities for agility. It is important to fix this, in order to compete in a dynamic environment

RESILIENCE AND RENEWAL

- **High, robust, balanced.** A high score means a robust organization with capabilities to withstand external shocks. The task is to maintain them at that level
- **Medium, limited.** With a medium score, the organization risks fighting new challenges with yet another project to fix the gaps. The task is to invest in resilient capabilities
- **Low, fragile.** A low score indicates a lack of any defensive mechanisms. With the smallest change or shock, the organization is at risk. The task is to invest in resilient capabilities, and to do so quickly

DYNAMIC CAPABILITIES

- **High, unrestrained.** A high score means well-developed dynamic capabilities with a high ability to act. The organization is fit for the future
- **Medium, missing.** A medium score means average dynamic capabilities. There is room for improvement with an investment in capabilities to address the future
- **Low, missing.** A low score means limited capabilities. Without an intervention to develop these capabilities, the organization risks losing its competitive edge

PERFORMANCE

- **Top.** A high score means people have the means to perform at their peak
- **Mediocre.** A medium score means inferences prevent people from using their full potential. Performance likely suffers
- **Missing or blocked.** A low score means people don't use their potential. They are bored, stressed or work in an infected environment

INNOVATION

- **Productive.** A high score means a prospering organization where ideas turn into action. The task is to build on the current management approach
- **Limited.** A medium score indicates an organization where the status quo prevails. New ideas take time to translate into action. Work *on* the system is needed
- **Missing or wasted.** A low score indicates a hesitant organization. It draws from the past with nothing new coming forward. The task is to fundamentally work *on* the system

GROWTH

- **Superior.** A high score means that the organization captures relevant opportunities. The task is to build on current capabilities
- **Maintaining.** A medium score indicates an organization that hardly moves. The task is to move out of the middle ground by reviewing capabilities
- **Missing.** A low score indicates an organization that loses market presence. The task is to review capabilities in order to change the current situation

OUTCOMES

- **Future-proof.** A high score means that the organization delivers superior outcomes with ongoing renewal and competitive advantages
- **Sustaining.** A medium score indicates partially supportive capabilities to sustain the future
- **Weak, missing.** A low score means that the organization misses the essentials to compete in the future

---

Next, use the Fitness Index from Figure 79 to identify your organization's agile maturity (Figure 80).

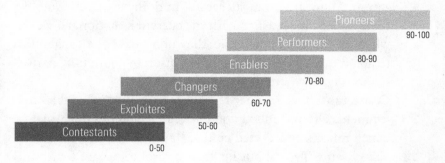

FIGURE 80: AGILE MATURITY

Here is what your agile maturity means:
- **Pioneers** have a design for continuous evolution. They use dynamic capabilities to deliver superior outcomes. Decentralized decision-making, teamwork and personal influence are the trademarks of a new way to manage – the agile way – with guided self-organization as one of its fundamental principles.
- **Performers** have a design for a dynamic environment. They've built the capabilities that enable them to navigate in a VUCA world, and that balance people's needs and organizational objectives. Lateral coordination, self-control and connectivity help them outdo peers, even in a turbulent context, on performance, innovation and growth.

- **Enablers** have a design for people engagement that works well in a stable environment. These organizations engage people based on self-responsibility, purpose and social control. They favour action-orientation and knowledge work. However, people-centric is insufficient in a dynamic setting. The fix is radically decentralized decision-making.
- **Changers** have a design for disruptive change. Whenever their leaders believe that change is required, they alter structures and reallocate resources. As the context changes, they keep restructuring. Their fix is always more control, direct managerial influence and relentless customer focus.
- **Exploiters** have a design for exploitation. They optimize processes to deliver at the lowest possible level of asset utilization. Many are quite successful in doing so. Consequently, their leaders are satisfied with the current situation. However, when markets turn dynamic, they don't have the capabilities to adapt quickly. They fix their situation by tightening performance management and embark on change.
- **Contestants** have an inherited design to operate in a stable environment. Often, context and current capabilities don't match, which reflects an infected culture, faulty leadership or erroneous systems. Typical but ineffective resolutions are fixing culture, people and leaders. Contestants are stuck in bureaucracy.

Finally, identify and mark your organization's Operating Mode (Figure 81).

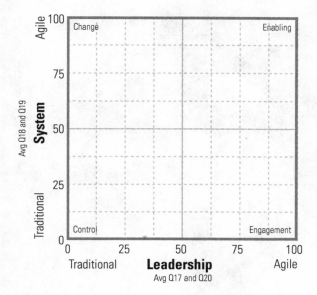

FIGURE 81: OPERATING MODE

Engage your team in the conversation with the following questions. Use the Canvas (Figure 82) as a poster or worksheet to list your answers.

- What are our current capabilities?
- What are our desired capabilities?
- What is our current and desired Agile Maturity?
- What are the elements that require our attention?
- What is our current and desired Operating Mode?
- What is the shift to develop People-Centric Management?
- What is our intervention path for the transformation?

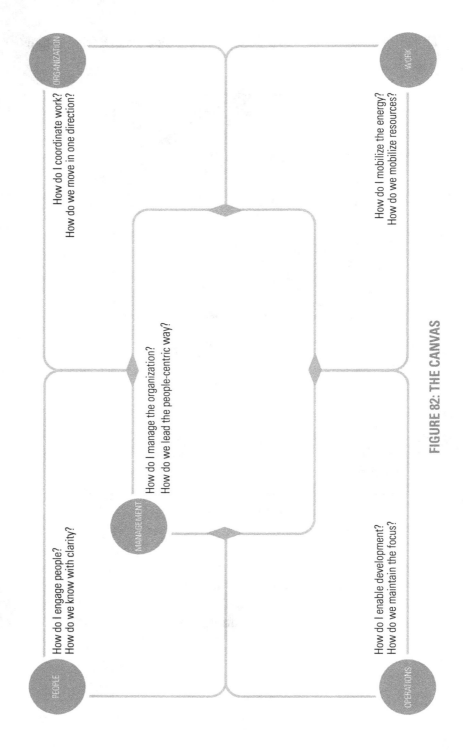

FIGURE 82: THE CANVAS

ORGANIZATION

How do I coordinate work?
How do we move in one direction?

WORK

How do I mobilize the energy?
How do we mobilize resources?

MANAGEMENT

How do I manage the organization?
How do we lead the people-centric way?

PEOPLE

How do I engage people?
How do we know with clarity?

OPERATIONS

How do I enable development?
How do we maintain the focus?

FURTHER READING & TOOLS

Nold, H; Anzengruber, J; Michel, L; and Wölfle, M (2018). Organizational Agility: Testing, Validity and Reliability of a Diagnostic Instrument. *Journal of Organizational Psychology,* 18(3).

A free online version of the AGILE SCAN is available on the AGILITYINSIGHTS website: https://agilityinsights.net/free-agile-scan

NOTES

1. **Dynamic capabilities.** Freely defined based on a variety of sources: Teece et al. (1997, page 516); Eisenhardt and Martin (2000, page 1107); Zollo and Winter (2002, pages 339-340); Zahra et al. (2006, page 918); Helfat et al. (2007, page 4); and more ...

2. **Context and management.** For a detailed discussion on the new context and its implications on management, read the scientific publication: Michel, L; Anzengruber, J; Wölfle, M; and Hixson, N (2018). Under What Conditions do Rules-Based and Capability-Based Management Modes Dominate? *Special Issue Risks in Financial and Real Estate Markets Journal,* 6(32).

3. **Knowledge workers.** See Drucker, PF (2006). *The Effective Executive: The Definitive Guide to Getting the Right Things Done.* New York: Harper Business Essentials.

4. **Learning.** See Senge, PM (1990). *The Fifth Discipline.* New York: Doubleday, 321.

5. **Systems.** See Scholtes, PR (1998). *The Leader's Handbook: Making Things Happen, Getting Things Done.* New York: McGraw-Hill, ix.

6. **The dynamic capabilities framework.** Originally developed by Teece, Pisano and Shuen (Teece and Pisano, 1994; Teece, Pisano and Shuen, 1997), and is now further developed with many new publications every year. It builds on theoretical foundations provided by Schumpeter (1934); Penrose (1959); Hamel and Prahalad (1994); and Turner and Crawford (1994).

7. **Change capacity.** For a detailed discussion, see Hayes et al. (1988); Prahalad and Hamel (1990); Chandler (1990); and Teece (1993).

8. **Diagnostics.** For more information, see https://agilityinsights.net (Last retrieved 30 March 2020.)

9. **Reflection.** Perspectives can be reached through a variety of different approaches, combining information, knowledge and power positions (Foucault, 1974, 1977; and Bruch and Türk, 2005).

10. **Traps.** Any observer is always subjected to individual interests, values, norms, power and relationships. Standardized capability assessments and multiple views help to reduce competence traps.

11. **Assessment.** Dynamic capabilities need to be derived from indicators (Easterby-Smith, Lyles and Peteraf, 2009).

12. **Observation.** Moldaschl (2007) offers the criteria for institutionalized observation and evaluation.

13. **Monitoring.** Through ongoing learning in the context of dynamic capabilities (Eisenhardt and Martin, 2000), and the continuous absorption of new environmental signals, organizations risk losing their ability to act. A cognitive overload and systems

overload are the results. As such, learning and change in the context between stability and agility happens within clear limits and require a supportive structure. And so, capability monitoring is an infrequent, non-routine event that uses existing knowledge and patterns to initiate the learning of new knowledge and behaviours (Luhmann, 1995).

14. **Politics.** It is the ongoing exchange and bargaining among all stakeholders in a firm about their goals, interests and values (Ulrich and Fluri, 1992), which includes power positions (Pfeffer, 1981; Schirmer, 2000; Hardy and Clegg, 2006). Organizations are not free from politics (e.g., from interests of actors), nor do they behave in an interest-free, consistent goal system or work towards one overall objective (Cyert and March, 1963; Pfeffer, 1981; Mintzberg, 1983). Organizations are usually seen as pluralistic social entities, with varying values, goals and interest conflicts between actors and groups. Consensus on legitimacy of values, goals and means to achieve goals (resource distribution, technologies, processes, structures) are not a given. They need to be agreed upon (Giddens, 1984).

15. **Reflection.** Observation is about capability monitoring and reflection is about the use of capability. However, separating the two resembles Frederic Taylor's separation of thinking and doing. To solve the separation problem, Schreyögg and Kliesch-Eberl (2007), propose separating observation from any routine and introducing institutionalized reflection.

16. **Learning.** It is always individual and requires supportive organizational structures to be effective. Individual memory develops by absorbing new knowledge and through the use of knowledge. New knowledge connects with existing knowledge and cognitive structures. The more that objects, patterns and concepts already exist in our brain, the easier it is to absorb new information and create new knowledge for existing topics (Cohen and Levinthal, 1990). This implies that learning in new fields is more difficult than in existing areas. For most people, agile is a new area. Effective learning in the context of work, especially to cope with the tension between stability and agility, requires a supportive learning environment.

17. **Perspectives.** Sense-making combines individual observation with institutional reflection, which are always preformed through organizational practices (Weick, 1995; Moldaschl, 2003). Awareness, observation and interpretation of actors lead to distancing, critique and dissent. "To talk about interpretation without discussing a politics of interpretation is to ignore context" (Weick, 1995). The team workshop helps participants reflect and share their points of view.

18. **Dissent.** Variety in perspectives and open conversations are important parts of capability monitoring (Schreyögg and Kliesch-Eberl, 2007) that can be used by participants for their interests (Crozier and Friedberg, 1979; Schirmer, 2003).

19. **Rules.** To ensure broad participation, one common language is a must. Conversations follow the practice of listening and only conducting one conversation at a time. Short interventions, and tolerance for diverging ideas and opinions, guide the discourse. Guided face-to-face meetings help to resolve conflicts. Mentors lead the conversation. And, additional rules can always be added.

20. **Interventions.** See Argyris (1990); Schein (1985); Zollo and Winter (2002).

BIBLIOGRAPHY

AGILITYINSIGHTS. (2018). *Agile Management Design – A Global Study on Agile Capabilities.* Download from www.agilityinsights.net.

Ansoff, H (1980). Strategic Issue Management. *Strategic Management Journal*, 1, 131-148.

Argyris, C (1990). *Overcoming Organizational Defenses.* Boston: Allyn and Bacon.

Beer, M; Finnström, M; and Schrader, D (2016). Why Leadership Training Fails – and What to Do About It. *Harvard Business Review,* October.

Beer, M and Eisenstat, RA (2004). How to Have an Honest Conversation About Your Business Strategy. *Harvard Business Review*, February.

Beer, M; Eisenstat, RA; and Spector, B (1990). Why Change Programs Don't Produce Change. *Harvard Business Review*, November-December.

Birkinshaw, J (2010). *Reinventing Management.* San Francisco, California: Jossey-Bass..

Bloom, N and van Reenen, J (2007). Measuring and Explaining Management Practices Across Firms and Countries. *The Quarterly Journal of Economics,* 122.4, 1351-1408.

Bruch, M and Türk, K (2005). Organisation als Regierungsdispositiv der modernen Gesellschaft. In Jäger, W; and Schimank, U. *Organisationsgesellschaft* (pp. 89-123). Wiesbaden: Verlag für Sozialwissenschaften.

Cohen, W and Levinthal, D (1990). Absorptive Capacity: A New Perspective on Learning and Innovation. *Administrative Science Quarterly* (35), 128-152.

Cyert, R and March, J (1963). *A Behavioral Theory of the Firm.* Englewood Cliffs, NJ: Prentice Hall.

Chandler, AD Jr. (1990). *Scale and Scope.* London: Belknap Press.

Christensen, CM (2015). *The Innovator's Dilemma: When New Technologies Cause Great Firms to Fail.* Boston: Harvard Business Review Press.

Crozier, M and Friedberg, E (1979). *Macht und Organization.* Königstein: Athensäum-Verlag.

Denning, S (2015). How to Make the Whole Organization Agile. *Forbes,* 22 July.

Dood, D and Favaro, K (2006). Managing the Right Tensions. *Harvard Business Review,* December.

Drucker, PF (1997). *Managing in a Time of Great Change.* Abingdon: Routledge.

Drucker, PF (2006). *The Effective Executive: The Definitive Guide to Getting the Right Things Done.* New York: Harper Business Essentials.

Dunning, D (2011). "The Dunning–Kruger Effect: On Being Ignorant of One's Own Ignorance." *Advances in Experimental Social Psychology*: 44, 247-296.

Edmondson, A (2018). *The Fearless Organization: Creating Psychological Safety in the Workplace for Learning, Innovation, and Growth.* Hoboken, New Jersey: Wiley.

Easterby-Smith, M and Prieto, I (2008). Dynamic Capabilities and Knowledge Management: An Integrative Role for Learning? *British Journal of Management,* 19 (3), 235-249.

Eisenhardt, K and Martin, JA (2000). Dynamic Capabilities: What are they? *Strategic Management Journal,* 21, 1105-1121.

Foucault, M (1977). *Überwachen und Strafen.* Frankfurt am Main: Suhrkamp.

Foucault, M (1974). *Die Ordnung der Dinge.* Frankfurt am Main: Suhrkamp.

Gallup.com (2020). State of the Global Workplace. Last accessed 16 March 2020. https://www.gallup.com/workplace/238079/state-global-workplace-2017.aspx.

Galford, R; and Drapeau, AS (2002). *The Trusted Leaders: Bringing out the Best in Your People and Your Company.* New York: The Free Press.

Gallwey, WT (2000). *The Inner Game of Work.* New York: Random House.

Gavrilova, T; Carlucci, D; and Schiuma, G (2013). Art of Visual Thinking for Smart Business Education. Proceedings of the 8th International Forum on Knowledge Asset Dynamics. Zagreb, Croatia: IFKAD, 12-14.

Giddens, A (1984). *The Constitution of Society.* Berkley: University of California Press.

Ghoshal, S (2005). Bad Management Theories Are Destroying Good Management Practices. *Academy of Management Learning & Education.* 4 (1) Pages 75-91.

Graves, CW (1970). Levels of Existence: An Open System Theory of Values. *Journal of Humanistic Psychology,* Fall.

Habermas, J (1988). *Moralbewusstsein und kommunikatives Handeln,* 3. Aufl. Frankfurt a M.

Hamel, G and Zanini, M (2016). Top-Down Solutions Like Holacracy Won't Fix Bureaucracy. *Harvard Business Review,* March.

Hamel, G (2007). *The Future of Management.* Boston: Harvard Business School Press.

Hamel, G (2006). The Why, What, and How of Management Innovation. *Harvard Business Review,* February.

Hamel, G (2000). *Leading the Revolution.* Boston, Harvard Business School Press.

Hamel, G and Prahalad, CK (1994). Competing for the Future. *Harvard Business Review.* July-August.

Hammer, M and Champy, J (1993). *Reengineering the Corporation,* HarperBusiness.

Handy, C (2019). *21 Letters on Life and its Challenges.* London: Hutchinson.

Hardy, C and Clegg, S (2006). Some Dare Call it Power. In Clegg, S; Hardy, C; Lawrence, T; and Nord, W (2006). *The SAGE Handbook of Organization Studies* (2nd ed., pp. 754-775). Thousand Oaks: Sage.

Hayes, RH; Wheelwright, SC; and Clark, KB (1988). *Dynamic Manufacturing: Creating the Learning Organization.* New York: The Free Press.

Heywood S; Spungin, J; and Turnball, D (2007). Cracking the Complexity Code. *McKinsey Quarterly,* 2.

Helfat, C; Finkelstein, S; Mitchell, W; Peteraf, M; Singh, H; Teece, D; and Winter, SG (2007). *Dynamic Capabilities: Understanding Strategic Change in Organizations.* Malden, Australia: Blackwell Publishing.

Hope, J and Fraser, R (2003). *Beyond Budgeting: How Managers Can Break Free From the Annual Performance Trap.* Boston, MA: Harvard Business School Press.

Hurst, DK (2018). *Lead Like a Gardener! Agile and Design Thinking will Become Fads Unless We Expand on the Concept of Management.* Medium.com, last modified 9 October 2018. *https://medium.com/@davidkhurst/lead-like-a-gardener-b4c6181af8e5:.*

Hurst, DK (2014). *The New Ecology of Leadership: Business Mastery in a Chaotic World.* New York: Columbia University Press.

Kahneman, D (2011). *Thinking, Fast and Slow.* USA: Macmillan.

Kay, J (2010). *Obliquity: Why Our Goals are Best Achieved Indirectly.* London: Profile Books.

Kleiner, A (2008). *The Age of Heretics: A History of the Radical Thinkers Who Reinvented Corporate Management.* San Francisco: Jossey-Bass.

Kotter, JP and Heskett, JL (1992). *Corporate Culture and Performance.* New York: Free Press.

Kotter, JP (1996). *Leading Change. Harvard Business Review Press.*

Kotter, JP (1995). Leading Change: Why Transformation Efforts Fail. *Harvard Business Review,* March-April, 59-67.

Laloux, F (2014). *Reinventing Organizations: A Guide to Creating Organizations Inspired by the Next Stage in Human Consciousness.* Nelson Parker.

Luhmann, N (1995). *Social Systems.* Stanford: Stanford University Press.

Martin, RL (2017). Use Design Thinking to Build Commitment to a New Idea. *Harvard Business Review,* January.

Meynhardt, T and Gomez, P (2013). Organizationen schöpfen Wert für die Gesellschaft. In: Heuser, J et al. *DIE ZEIT erklärt die Wirtschaft* (199–207). Hamburg: Murmann.

Meadows, D (2001). Dancing with Systems – Tools Ideas Environment. Initially published by *Whole Earth Review,* www.wholeearth.com. Accessible through http://donellameadows.org/archives/dancing-with-systems/.

Michel, L; Anzengruber, J; Wölfle, M; and Hixson, N (2018). Under What Conditions do Rules-Based and Capability-Based Management Modes Dominate? *Special Issue Risks in Financial and Real Estate Markets Journal,* 6(32).

Michel, L (2020). *Agile by Choice: How You Can Make the Shift to Establish Leadership Everywhere.* London: LID Publishing.

Michel, L (2017). *Management Design: Managing People and Organizations in Turbulent Times* (Second ed.). London: LID Publishing.

Michel, L (2013). *The Performance Triangle: Diagnostic Mentoring to Manage Organizations and People for Superior Performance in Turbulent Times.* London: LID Publishing.

Michel, L (2013). The Performance Triangle: A Diagnostic Tool to Help Leaders Translate Knowledge into Action for Higher Agility. *Organizational Cultures: An International Journal*, 12(2), 13-28.

Mintzberg, H (1983). *Power In and Around Organizations.* Englewood Cliffs: Prentice Hall.

Moldaschl, M (2007), No. 2. *Institutional Reflexivity. An Institutional Approach to Measure Innovativeness of Firms.* Papers and Reprints of the Department of Innovation Research and Sustainable Resource Management. Wiesbaden: Gabler.

Moldaschl, M (2003). Foucaults Brille. In *Moldaschl, Subjektivierung von Arbeit* (pp. 135-177). Munich: Hampp.

Nayar, V (2010). *Employees First, Customers Second.* Boston: Harvard Business School Press.

Nelson, RR and Winter, SG (1982). *An Evolutionary Theory of Economic Change.* Cambridge MA and London: Belknap Press of Harvard University Press.

Nold, H (2018). Dynamic Capabilities for People-Centric Management in Turbulent Times. *Dark Sides of Organizational Behavior and Leadership.* IntechOpen.

Nold, H; Anzengruber, J; Michel, L; and Wölfle, M (2018). Organizational Agility: Testing, Validity and Reliability of a Diagnostic Instrument. *Journal of Organizational Psychology,* 18(3).

Nold, H and Michel, L (2016). The Performance Triangle: A Model for Corporate Agility. *Leadership & Organizational Development Journal,* 37(3).

O'Reilly, CA and Tushman, ML (2004). The Ambidextrous Organization. *Harvard Business Review,* April.

Penrose, ET (1959). *The Theory of the Growth of the Firm.* New York: Wiley.

Pfeffer, J and Sutton, RI (2000). *The Knowing-Doing Gap: How Smart Companies Turn Knowledge into Action.* Harvard Business School Press.

Pfeffer, J (1998). *The Human Equation: Building Profits by Putting People First.* Boston, Harvard Business School Press.

Pfeffer, J (1981). *Power in Organizations.* Marshfield: Pitman Publishing.

Prahalad, CK and Hamel, G (1990). The Core Competence of the Corporation. *Harvard Business Review,* May-June.

Robertson, BJ (2015). *Holacracy: The Revolutionary Management System that Abolishes Hierarchy.* New York: Penguin.

Salo, O in McKinsey (2017). *How to Create an Agile Organization.* Survey report.

Schein, EH (1985). *Organizational Culture and Leadership: A Dynamic View.* San Francisco: Wiley.

Schreyögg, G and Kliesch-Eberl, M (2007). How Dynamic Can Organizational Capabilities Be? Towards a Dual-Processs Model of Capability Dynamization. *Strategic Management Journal,* 28, 913-933.

Schreyögg, G and Noss, C (2000). Reframing Change in Organizations: The Equilibrium Logic and Beyond. Academy of Management: Best Paper Proceedings, Toronto, August.

Schumpeter, J (1934). *The Theory of Economic Development.* Cambridge, MA: Harvard University Press.

Schirmer, F (2000). *Reorganisationsmanagement. Interessenkonflikte. Koalitionen des Wandels und Reorganisationserfolg.* Wiesbaden: Deutscher Universitätsverlag.

Schirmer, F (2003). *Mobilisierung von Koalitionen für den Wandel in Organisationen.* In DBW (Vol. 63, 23-42).

Scholtes, PR (1998). *The Leader's Handbook: Making Things Happen, Getting Things Done.* New York: McGraw-Hill.

Scocco, A (2008). *Costruire mappe per rappresentare e organizzare il proprio pensiero.* Franco Angeli.

Senge, PM (1990). *The Fifth Discipline.* New York: Doubleday.

Simon, HA (1957). *Administrative Behavior.* New York: The Free Press.

Simons, R (2005). *Levers of Organization Design: How Managers use Accountability Systems for Greater Performance and Commitment.* Boston: Harvard Business School Press.

Simons, R and Dávila, A (1998). How High is Your Return on Management? *Harvard Business Review,* January-February.

Simons, R (1995). *Levers of Control: How Managers use Innovative Control Systems to Drive Strategic Renewal.* Boston: Harvard Business School Press.

Sowa, JF Jr. (1984). *Conceptual Structures: Information Processing in Mind and Machine.* Reading, MA: Addison-Wesley.

Stacey, RD (2000). *Complexity and Management.* New York, NY: Routledge.

Sull, D; Homkes R; and Sull, C (2015). Why Strategy Execution Unravels — and What to Do About It. *Harvard Business Review,* March.

Sutton, RI (2014). Eight Essentials for Scaling Up Without Screwing Up. *Harvard Business Review,* February.

Sprenger, RK (2010). *Mythos Motivation: Wege aus der Sackgasse.* Campus. Erweiterte Auflage.

Sprenger, RK (2007). *Vertrauen führt: Worauf es im Unternehmen wirklich ankommt.* Frankfurt/New York: Campus. 3 Auflage.

Sprenger, RK (2007). *Das Prinzip Selbstverantwortung: Wege zur Motivation.* Frankfurt/New York: Campus.

Teece, D; Pisano, G; and Shuen, A (1997). Dynamic Capabilities and Strategic Management. *Strategic Management Journal,* 509-533.

Teece, D and Pisano, G (1994). The Dynamic Capabilities of Firms: An Introduction. *Industrial and Corporate Change,* 3(3), 537-556.

Teece, D (1993). The Dynamics of Industrial Capitalism: Perspectives on Alfred Chandler's Scale and Scope. *Journal of Economic Literature,* 31(1), 199-225. Retrieved from www.jstor.org/stable/2728154.

Turner, D and Crawford, M (1994). Managing Current and Future Competitive Performance: The Role of Competences. In Hamel, G and Heene, A (Eds.). *Competence-based Competition* (pp. 241-254). New York: John Wiley & Sons.

Ulrich, D; and Smallwood, N (2004). Capitalizing on Capabilities. *Harvard Business Review,* June.

Ulrich, P; and Fluri, E (1992). *Management* (6. neubearbeitete und ergänzte Auflage ed.). Bern: Haupt.

Von Krogh, G; Ichijo, K; and Nonaka, IO (2000). *Enabling Knowledge Creation – How to Unlock the Mystery of Tacit Knowledge and Release the Power of Innovation.* Oxford: University Press.

Von Foerster, H (1984). *Observing Systems.* Seaside, CA: Intersystems Publication.

Weber, M (1978 [1928]). Bureaucracy. In Roth, RG and Wittich, C (Eds.). *Economy and Society* (S. 956-980). Berkeley, CA: University of California Press.

Weick, K (1995). *Sensemaking in Organizations.* Thousand Oaks, CA: Sage Publications.

Wüthrich, HA; Osemtz, D; and Kaduk, S (2006). *Musterbrecher: Führung neu erleben [Braking Patterns: How Leaders Re-experience Leadership].* Wiesbaden: Gabler.

Zahra, SA; Sapienza, HP; and Davidsson, P (2006). Entrepreneurship and Dynamic Capabilities: a Review, Model and Research Agenda. *Journal of Management Studies,* 43(4), 917-955.

Zollo, M and Winter, SG (2002). Deliberate Learning and the Evolution of Dynamic Capabilities. *Organization Science,* 13(3), 339-351.

LIST OF FIGURES

ABOUT THE AUTHOR

Lukas Michel is the owner of Agility Insights AG, based in Switzerland, and CEO of AGILITYINSIGHTS.NET, a global network of experienced business mentors.

In addition to lecturing at universities, licencing his own agile mentoring methodology, writing on management issues and building his consulting network, Lukas is a business leader with a track record of balance sheet accountability in his work for global corporations in Europe and Asia.

Over the course of his 40-year career he has worked with executive teams around the world, focusing on management and agility for a diverse range of local, national and global organizations.

For the last 20 years Lukas has been developing Diagnostic Mentoring, the methodology that offers diagnostics and a common framework and language for scaling 'agile' capabilities across all organizational levels.

He holds a master's degree in management from North Carolina State University, and bachelor's degrees in textile management and teaching.

Lukas is the author of *The Performance Triangle*, *Management Design*, *Agile by Choice* and *People-Centric Management*.

BOOK SUMMARY

Today's dynamic business environment requires new ways to manage, lead, work, and organize. Traditional paradigms of efficiency, agency theory, transactions and scale are replaced or augmented with principles that focus on people, self-organization, and purpose for greater innovation and growth.

To expand on his previous books, Lukas Michel presents new research, practical applications and the experience with People-Centric Management, agile organization and work *on* the system to establish new management where people unlock their talent, master greater challenges and perform at their peak.

The book offers the legendary People-Centric Diagnostic that forces the reader to decode and rethink the many assumptions underlying their management model and systems. In combination, the people-centric model, the three-step process and action agenda will help executives establish leadership everywhere to succeed in a dynamic environment.

CPSIA information can be obtained
at www.ICGtesting.com
Printed in the USA
JSHW031025311220
10665JS00002B/50

9 781912 555994